To

From

Date

STORIES TO
WARM THE HEART
AT
Christmas

True Stories of Hope and Inspiration

EDITED BY JAMES STUART BELL

Guideposts

Stories to Warm the Heart at Christmas

ISBN-10: 0-8249- 4936-6
ISBN-13: 978-0-8249-4936-5

Published by Guideposts
16 East 34th Street
New York, New York 10016
Guideposts.org

Distributed by Ideals Publications, a Guideposts company
2630 Elm Hill Pike, Suite 100
Nashville, Tennessee 37214

Guideposts and *Ideals* are registered trademarks of Guideposts.

Cover and interior design by Thinkpen Design, Inc., www.thinkpendesign.com
Cover art/photo by Shutterstock
Typeset by Thinkpen Design, Inc.

Printed and bound in China
10 9 8 7 6 5 4 3 2 1

Contents

Introduction vii

A Surprise for Andy *by Nancy George* 1

Christmas Within *by Frances E. Wilson* 7

Director's Cut *by Catherine Hardwicke* 11

Trouble at the Inn *by Dina Donohue* 18

An Unusual Year *by Christian Dornbierer* 22

On the Way to Christmas *by Mala Powers* 26

Firstborn *by Linda Ching Sledge* 31

Christmas Found *by Jacqueline Ziarko Werth* 36

Ten Precious Minutes *by Nelson Sousa* 42

The Stocking *by Jim Hinch* .50

A Christmas House *by Brian Jones* 56

Ugly the Beautiful *by Faye Roberts* 62

Christmas 1914 *Author Unknown* 69

A Christmas Crisis *by Melva Vandiver* 72

Keeping Christmas *by Dorothy Walworth* 78

A Portion of Thyself *by Robert Halverson* 84

A Long Way Home *by Maria Didrichsons* 90

The Quiet People *by the Editors of Guideposts* 98

Christmas in Kuling *by Katherine Paterson*. 104

In Full Supply *by Jacqueline Hewitt Allen* 109

The Old Steamer Trunk *by Sarah Hudson-Pierce* 115

When Time Stood Still *by Adela Rogers St. Johns* 119

At Christmas Town *by Sam McGarrity*. 124

A "Sensible" Christmas *by Henry Appers*. 132

The Christmas Expedition *by Alexander Ness* 139

Gold, Circumstance, & Mud *by Rex Knowles* 148

Adele *by Ned Waldman* 151

Stop, Look, & Listen *by Sue Monk Kidd* 155

A Time for Imagination *by Comtesse M. De La Riviere* 159

A Very English Christmas *by Barbara Hampton*. 162

Our Light in the Night *by Margaret Pegram Morrison* 168

Shining Through *by Shari Smyth* 172

Empty Manger *by Mary Ann O'Roark* 179

Introduction

Nothing evokes the nostalgia, the sense of wonder and longing, and the richest sights, sounds and smells, as Christmas does. It's a time when it's frosty outside but warm with the glow of bright lights, freshly baked cookies, and glowing embers below stockings hung with care. But most of all, it's the warmth in our hearts—for the newborn Savior, for family and friends, and for those who are less fortunate.

Here is a volume of stories with The Greatest Story Ever Told always in the background. Christmas is a time of drama—literally and figuratively. Will my daughter perform okay in the nativity play? Will I get that last present on Christmas Eve before the stores close? Will my son and daughter-in-law be restored at the family gathering? What about that homeless man with nowhere to go? These are stories where God moves in mysterious ways, stories not only filled with the season's delights, but richly endowed with spiritual meaning, ties to the past, and dreams for the future.

There are unexpected twists and surprise endings to these Christmas stories; every year the traditions continue but something new emerges. In "The Christmas Crisis," Melva Vandiver says: "Future Christmases will be easier now, thanks to Mom. And the feeling of loneliness has gone.... Christian love has pushed out the anger inside us." That, indeed, is the message of Christmas. The appearance of Someone who can reconcile us to Himself and to each other. Someone who can take away our loneliness and anger and hurt.

Yes, the Christmas spirit can be felt throughout these stories; and as we let that spirit enter our hearts, the warm glow will be felt by others near and far.

A Surprise for Andy

Tree-trimming day was a big deal in our family, but not this Christmas, not with Andy, my youngest, so sick. I brought in a big, full-branched tree that reached almost to the ceiling, hoping it would cheer him up. Hoping it would cheer all of us up. I put on some holiday music. Emily, twelve, and Adam, eight, strung the lights and hung the ornaments. Four-year-old Andy tried to help. But after hanging a few strands of tinsel, he lay on the couch, too weak to do anything besides watch.

His doctors told me to keep his life as normal as possible. But how? How could I forget the row of medicine bottles on the kitchen counter? The rough-and-tumble, impossible-to-keep-up-with boy my little son had been just ten months earlier? So much had changed so quickly for us.

Andy was my Energizer bunny. He didn't just start walking early, he ran...racing to do everything his big brother and sister did. Fearless. He was constantly getting bumps and bruises. At age two he made the first of many visits to the ER, to get stitches on his finger. Maybe that was why I hadn't been all that worried on Valentine's Day when his preschool teacher told me he'd been limping. "He fell down a couple of times too," Mrs. Strong said at morning pickup.

I sighed and shot my rambunctious little one a look. "I bet he hurt himself jumping off the playhouse again." Andy liked to climb onto the roof of our backyard playhouse and leap off. "But I'm a Power Ranger," he'd protested when I caught him at it the last time. I'd told him in no uncertain terms to stay off that roof, but there was no telling with Andy.

"I'll keep an eye on him," I told Mrs. Strong. I noticed a little hitch in his stride as we walked to the car, but he was moving as fast as usual, so I figured it would soon go away.

We stopped by Emily and Adam's school to help with their Valentine's Day class parties. Andy was thrilled to be included, but by the end of the afternoon, his limp was worse, and he asked me to carry him. Something was very wrong. Andy couldn't stand being babied.

I took him to the pediatrician. Dr. Fernandez suspected Andy had a hip infection, and he ordered blood tests. "We'll have the results in a few hours," he said.

I knew it was bad when Dr. Fernandez himself, not a nurse, called back. "Andy seems so healthy that I ran the tests twice just to be sure," he said. "This isn't an infection. It's more serious, Mrs. George." And I guess that's when everything changed—my whole world shifted on its axis. Dr. Fernandez suspected Andy had leukemia.

"Go to the emergency room at Children's Medical Center," he said. "They're expecting you."

Children's Medical Center was only a half hour drive. Thanks to Andy, I knew the way, of course. Still, I was so frazzled that I kept making wrong turns. Finally we got there. A nurse hustled us into an examining room. She pulled the curtain and took out a needle to draw blood. Andy crawled into my lap and started to cry. So did I. The nurse took me aside. "It won't help him to see you cry," she whispered. "You have to pull yourself together for him."

I took a deep breath and managed to quell my tears for Andy's sake, but I fell apart again as soon as the tests confirmed the diagnosis: acute lymphocytic leukemia. The best treatment, the doctors said, was an aggressive course of chemotherapy.

Andy got the drugs both intravenously and through spinal taps. I didn't know which was worse, my son wailing, his face, his whole body, clenched with fear, or barely speaking because he was so sick from the chemotherapy treatment. I slept on a cot next to his hospital bed, praying that the treatment would work and trying not to let him hear me cry.

Every eight weeks we'd head to the hospital for another round of chemo. Then, because the drugs depleted his immune system, he'd have to stay home from preschool for two weeks until he regained some strength. No more racing around after Emily and Adam. No more Power Ranger. What I wouldn't give to see Andy try to defy gravity and fly off the roof of the playhouse again!

Each time he was allowed to go back to school it was like starting all over again. He was tentative, afraid. "I don't want to go to school," he said one day. By then most of his hair had fallen out. "What if all the kids there laugh at me?"

I stroked his few remaining blond wisps. "Mrs. Strong can't wait to see you," I said. "Remember how much you like her? You'll have fun." *Please, Lord, let that be true*, I added silently, knowing that four-year-olds tended to live in the moment and his classmates might not have thought of him at all now that they didn't see him every day.

At the doorway to his classroom, Andy hung back. "Go ahead," I urged. "Go play." Then a boy named Cubby came running up. "Hey, Andy's back!" he shouted. Without a moment's hesitation, he grabbed Andy's hand and pulled him over to the toys. I let out a breath I hadn't realized I'd been holding.

As his doctors had told me, being with his friends and getting back to his normal routine did Andy good. But leukemia didn't take a break for the holidays. So neither could we. Even though it was the week before Christmas, he still had to go in for chemo treatments.

That's why he was lying on the couch, pale and listless, only able to watch while the rest of us trimmed the tree. He wasn't the only one who was wiped out. I was so drained from the past ten months that even our favorite holiday ritual felt like a chore. The doctors said Andy's latest blood tests were encouraging, but they warned me it was too soon to tell whether he was out of the woods.

What if the next rounds of treatment didn't take, or he was so weakened by them he succumbed to infection? What if this turned out to be Andy's last Christmas?

The next day around lunchtime the doorbell rang. Mrs. Strong stood on the stoop, holding a big red bag with stickers on it. "Can I come in?" she asked. "I have something for Andy."

She followed me into the living room and knelt beside the couch where Andy was resting. "We've been making Christmas ornaments in school," Mrs. Strong said. "When I told your friends you wouldn't be in, they wanted to make these for you." She handed him the bag.

Andy opened it and took out the ornaments. There were silver bells made of aluminum foil. A Christmas ball that was a section of egg carton painted and covered with glitter. One child had made a wreath out of felt and sequins, another, a construction-paper tree decorated with confetti. Andy's face lit up. He got up from the couch and walked slowly to the tree with the ornaments. One by one, he took them by their pipe-cleaner hooks and hung them on the lowest branches. Then he turned to me. "Do you like them, Mom?" he asked me.

"I love them," I whispered, going over to Andy and taking him in my arms. *Thank You, Lord, for Andy, and for this Christmas.* There would be more chemo sessions and more nights at the hospital, but nothing could take away this feeling of being hoped for and cared for. My eyes filled with tears. The same tears of joy—and gratitude—that come now when I see those handmade ornaments, colors faded, sequins missing, in their place of honor by the angel that tops our Christmas tree, hung with care in the uppermost branches by my tall, healthy sixteen-year-old son Andy.

A Christmas Wish

I wish for you a happy Christmas. I wish you gifts that are beyond price, outlast time, and bridge all space. I wish you laughter and pure joy, a merry heart and love.... Most of all, I wish that the spirit of Christmas may draw you into companionship with the Giver of all gifts.

BISHOP REMINGTON

Christmas Within

BY FRANCES E. WILSON

Not light the star for Christmas! Why, that's unthinkable!" I said. I shook my head, finding it very hard to believe my husband really meant that we were not to have Christmas lights for outside decoration this year.

"We should do our part in conserving energy," he kept on insisting.

"But, Tom, our star is a tradition of over twenty years!" I argued. I felt unwilling to accept his attitude. My husband knew how important it was to me to keep our customs intact. I so look forward to this time of the year because it brings the whole family home together for the holidays. Like so many families, we had started many special Christmas traditions when our two children were infants. These continued from year to year and were a meaningful ritual to be carried out in our Yule celebration. The two most important of these customs for us were the placing of the nativity figures on the table in the family room and the hanging of the large silver star on the high cave at the front of the house. This star had been made for us by a dear friend. It contained sockets at each of the five points of the star and one in its center; these held round, blue light bulbs. Since these bulbs were larger and more powerful than the regular Christmas lights, they did, I realized, use more electricity. Even so, I continued to protest.

"I just can't see why using enough power for those lights on the star can have that much bearing on the energy shortage," I said.

"Now, Fran," Tom said in exasperation, "you know better than that."

"Well, surely if we give up the string of colored lights from around the front doorway and also the one we usually wind around the post of the lantern at the edge of the driveway, that will save enough. Then we can still have our star lighted!"

"I know our house using just one group of outside lights may not seem vital, but multiply that by thousands of homes and it is crucial!" Tom insisted. "Who knows, if we follow my plan we could just set an example for the whole neighborhood. Everybody needs to face the fact that energy conservation is necessary." The determined set of his jaw as he spoke emphasized his words. There could be no doubt, my husband was adamant about this.

I frowned at him and made no attempt to hide my disappointment. I knew I should try to be logical and reasonable, but instead I pressed my lips together in a pout.

"It won't be right—Christmas with an unlighted star," I said glumly. "When the family arrives for the holidays, what will they think? Just how will they feel when there are no outside lights to greet them?"

Tom reached over and patted my shoulder. "Christmas is not outside, Fran. It's inside where it counts. You'll see—you won't even miss the star when you get all your decorations up inside the house. The family will have the crèche as always, and that's our most important tradition."

I put my disappointment from my mind and busied myself with the decorations for inside the house. Lifting the box containing the nativity figures from the shelf, I carried it into the family room. Tom was right, the nativity was our loveliest custom and every member of the family treasured it. When Douglas and Pamela had been in grade school, their grandmother had brought this gift to us from the Holy Land. The interesting figures had been carved by a craftsman in Jerusalem. The mellow olive wood had a warm brown color with lines of darker wood grain running through it. The real beauty of these figures lay in the simplicity of the carving and the natural beauty of the wood. There were twelve in all: the infant Christ, Mary, Joseph, three wise men, two shepherds, two sheep, and a pair of oxen. Through the years we added a camel carved from a lighter-colored wood and also a charming small angel.

Tom's hobby is woodwork. Some years ago, he had turned on his wood lathe several candleholders of various heights made from cherry, walnut, and maple wood. These hold tall green candles and form an effective background for the crèche.

I had just arranged the figures of Mary and Joseph in their place beside the Christ child, and now I stepped back to view the completed setting. I decided to light the candles. In just a second the flames lengthened and burned with a steady, radiant glow.

An all-encompassing feeling of joy surrounded me and I thought, *Tom is right! The important part of Christmas is not to be seen outside but rather felt inside.* But it was even more than what Tom had meant. It is true that Christmas is not a string of colored outside lights or a lighted silver star, but neither is it tinsel and greenery inside a house. Christmas is the remembering—the knowing deep within each one of us that its real meaning is the birth of Jesus Christ our Savior.

I stood quietly gazing at the nativity scene—the simple olive-wood figures touched by a beautiful halo of candlelight. I felt elation. I felt Christmas within me.

The Real Meaning

You don't need candlelight and fireside glow to make Christmas happen. Trees, ornaments, gifts, and all of it are splendid embellishments. Not necessary, but so very nice. It's Him. He's finding more and more opened inns these days. It's priceless to discover the pleasure of His company.... May your home know something of all this glory during these days.

JACK HAYFORD

Director's Cut

High in the night sky a bright star shone down upon the humble stable. Inside, cows and sheep huddled for warmth, gazing curiously at the evening's unexpected guests: two young travelers from a distant village and their newborn child, who slumbered peacefully in a straw-filled manger. In the doorway, people quietly gathered to witness the event. For a brief moment, all was still and serene. Then the baby woke up and started to wail. A cow, startled, bolted for the door. The sheep baaed loudly. A donkey kicked up straw everywhere. Everyone turned toward me. I shook my head. "Cut!" I yelled.

On the set of *The Nativity Story*, one miraculous night of Jesus' birth was taking two nights to film, and we still weren't close to getting it perfect. The Bethlehem we recreated in the Italian countryside looked great. But that was about the only thing that had gone right. I stared at our local "expert" animal wrangler, trying in vain to get the creatures under control. The day before, he'd admitted to me that he'd never worked with farm animals. *Now you tell me*, I thought. Earlier in the day, the donkey Mary and Joseph rode fell and skinned its knee, and its understudy didn't look quite the same. So much for continuity.

Now, time was running out. The baby playing Jesus could only work for twenty-five minutes at a time, and only until midnight. It was already 11:15 p.m. And tomorrow we had to fly to Morocco to shoot the final scene. I sighed. *Are we ever going to get it right?*

I closed my eyes and pictured the perfect scene I wanted—like the *nacimiento* my family and I built in my childhood home every Christmas. It was a custom we picked up from the Latino families living around us in the town of McAllen, on the border in south Texas. I stacked old shoe boxes to make the stable, crumpled paper grocery bags to make the rocks and hills, and stretched Spanish moss to decorate the landscape, fashioning a Bethlehem that took up half of our living room. Then we added some figures of Mary, Joseph, the three wise men, the baby Jesus, and the barn animals. The only misbehaving creatures back then were our cats, who hid behind the manger and batted at the hanging moss. My dad sang at church and invited the whole choir to the house. We stood in front of the scene, singing carols late into the night.

I loved building those nativity scenes. In fact, after college I moved to Los Angeles and became a production designer, creating sets for films. I worked on twenty Hollywood movies. I hoped to one day make my own film. But I never imagined I'd make *The Nativity Story*. I was struggling to even get anybody interested in supporting my first movie. That is, until a thirteen-year-old girl named Nikki changed everything.

I'd known Nikki since she was five years old. Her mother was a good friend of mine in L.A., a hairdresser who cut my hair at their house whenever I came back from long movie shoots. One spring day I went there for the usual. We chatted as my friend busily snipped my bangs. Then the door flew open. Nikki stormed in. I'd watched her grow up over the years, but I was stunned at how different she looked since I'd last seen her. Where were the pigtails and overalls? Instead, she wore heavy make-up and tight clothes; her tongue and belly button were pierced. The tension between her and her mother was obvious. Nikki stomped down the hall into her room and slammed the door. What's going on?

"I don't know what to do," my friend said.

"Let me talk to her," I said. It wasn't easy—it took me months of spending time with Nikki, engaging her in fun activities like surfing, going to museums, and painting, before she finally began to open up. It was tough being a teenager in L.A.; she felt so much pressure to fit in that she woke at four thirty in the morning to do her hair and make-up, and she was only in seventh grade! She didn't grow up with the faith that I had, either, and she filled that void by hanging out with other troubled kids. She picked up some of their behavior. "What do you want to do with your life?" I asked.

"Be an actress," she confided. *Oh no, that's the worst thing,* I thought. But at least it would provide some focus. I took her to acting classes, bought her books on technique and method. The more we talked, the more I realized many teenage girls could relate to her story. What if we wrote a movie together about her experiences? Nikki agreed to do it. We wrote our screenplay in six days and made our movie, *Thirteen*, on a low budget. Nikki starred and I directed. It was therapy for Nikki. Her mom was there every day on the set, and the two of them became closer than ever. The film debuted to rave reviews. Scripts were sent to me by studios and agents, asking me to direct. I did another film, *Lords of Dogtown*, also about troubled kids. I was offered a bunch of cookie-cutter teen flicks, even one starring the Olsen twins. Then one day I was sent a script titled *The Nativity Story*. Memories of those nacimientos in McAllen flooded back.

But directing the story of Jesus' birth? I picked up the script, sat down, and started to read. The storyline focused on Mary's point of view, and quickly I realized how much of a mystery Mary was to me. All those years in Sunday school, we learned remarkably little about the mother of our Savior. After reading the script, I got on the computer and did some research. I was shocked to discover that many scholars believed Mary was thirteen when she became pregnant. Thirteen? I thought about Nikki at that age. How would a teenage Mary have dealt with the pressures of her time? This was a movie I was excited to do.

We couldn't film in Israel, so we settled on Morocco and Italy. We rebuilt Nazareth stone by stone in the Italian countryside, basing our work on the latest archaeological findings. A group of biblical re-enactors from Israel and a Jewish scholar came to teach the cast and crew about life in the Holy Land two millennia ago—how they built their houses, sheared sheep, sowed crops, baked bread, and made cheese. "People then didn't even pray the same way we do," said the scholar. "Rather than fold their hands and bow their heads, they were encouraged to create personal gestures to feel closer to God, like reaching their arms up to the heavens." When the angel Gabriel appeared to Mary, it's likely that she wasn't overly surprised; the supernatural was a part of people's everyday spiritual lives.

The cast and crew belonged to all different religions, but learning these things got everyone talking about their own faiths and where they connected. It was magical. Then shooting began, and the magic started to fade. Every scene we'd shot so far had been a struggle, and now the most important one, the scene in the stable, wasn't happening.

I looked at our Mary, a sixteen-year-old actress, sitting uncomfortably in the straw. Before the shoot, I had talked to her about what could have gone through the real Mary's mind when she found herself in this scene. Mary was just a teenager, experiencing the pain of childbirth, far from home in dire conditions. How did she deal with it? Up above the stable we had set up a bright light—the shining star above Bethlehem. "It wasn't only a signal to the three wise men, it was a reminder to Mary that she was connected to God," I explained. She could have doubted a miracle, especially after being turned away at every door and finding herself in a dirty stable. But she had faith it was all part of God's plan. And in that moment her faith was rewarded.

All during the shoot, I had tried to stay true to Scripture. Now I had to stay true to Mary's example. I calmed myself and focused on ways to fix the problems so we could get things done before midnight. A baby doll for over-the-shoulder shots. Moving some of the rowdier animals out of the frame.

"Okay, let's try it again," I said to the crew. Everyone got in position. Joseph and Mary knelt in the straw. Behind them, the trainer guided the animals into place. Baby Jesus was handed carefully to Mary. "Action," I said softly.

The cameras whirled. Baby Jesus nestled quietly in Mary's arms. The proud parents beamed and the shepherds gazed in wonder; even the animals seemed stilled, for a moment, by awe. Our own little miracle, looking—I hoped—not unlike the one that happened two thousand years ago.

The last difficult scene to shoot was with Mary and Joseph, their newborn in tow, escaping Bethlehem, on their way through the desert toward Galilee, where they would raise their child. Sandstorms in Morocco delayed our schedule. Once again, every shot became a race against the clock. Our last day, the temperature was well over 120 degrees, and our donkey Gilda refused to move. "Pull her!" I shouted to our Joseph.

"I am pulling on her," he insisted. Frustrated, we tried coaxing the donkey with treats. She still wouldn't budge. "We're running out of time to get this shot," our director of photography told me.

I thought about how hard the nativity scene had been. And what the Jewish scholar had told us about Mary's faith. Prayer was personal. People back then expected something supernatural, a miracle. I had an idea. I called together the crew and they all stood around in a circle. "I want everyone to concentrate. Pray that the donkey will walk." The crew eyed me skeptically. "Just roll camera, and when I say 'action,' pray." We set up the shot again. "Action!"

For a moment, all was still. Then the donkey took a timid step forward. Then another. And slowly the young family made their winding way toward the horizon, toward safety and deliverance into Egypt, the perfect ending to a first chapter of the story that reverberates through our lives today.

God With Us

Behold, the virgin shall be with child,
and bear a Son,
and they shall call His name Immanuel,
which is translated, "God with us."

MATTHEW 1:23 NKJV

Trouble at the Inn

BY DINA DONOHUE

For years now whenever Christmas pageants are talked about in a certain little town in the Midwest, someone is sure to mention the name of Wallace Purling. Wally's performance in one annual production of the nativity play has slipped into the realm of legend. But the old-timers who were in the audience that night never tire of recalling exactly what happened.

Wally was nine that year and in the second grade, though he should have been in the fourth. Most people in town knew that he had difficulty in keeping up. He was big and clumsy, slow in movement and mind. Still, Wally was well liked by the other children in his class, all of whom were smaller than he, though the boys had trouble hiding their irritation when Wally would ask to play ball with them, or any game, for that matter, in which winning was important.

Most often they'd find a way to keep him out, but Wally would hang around anyway—not sulking, just hoping. He was always a helpful boy, a willing and smiling one, and the natural protector, paradoxically, of the underdog. Sometimes if the older boys chased the younger ones away, it would always be Wally who'd say, "Can't they stay? They're no bother."

Wally fancied the idea of being a shepherd with a flute in the Christmas pageant that year, but the play's director, Miss Lumbard, assigned him to a more important role. After all, she reasoned, the Innkeeper did not have too many lines, and Wally's size would make his refusal of lodging to Joseph more forceful.

And so it happened that the usual large, partisan audience gathered for the town's yearly extravaganza of crooks and crèches, of beards, crowns, halos, and a whole stageful of squeaky voices. No one on stage or off was more caught up in the magic of the night than Wallace Purling. They said later that he stood in the wings and watched the performance with such fascination that from time to time Miss Lumbard had to make sure he didn't wander onstage before his cue.

Then the time came when Joseph appeared, slowly, tenderly guiding Mary to the door of the inn. Joseph knocked hard on the wooden door set into the painted backdrop. Wally the Innkeeper was there, waiting.

"What do you want?" Wally said, swinging the door open with a brusque gesture.

"We seek lodging."

"Seek it elsewhere." Wally looked straight ahead but spoke vigorously. "The inn is filled."

"Sir, we have asked everywhere in vain. We have traveled far and are very weary."

"There is no room in this inn for you." Wally looked properly stern.

"Please, good innkeeper, this is my wife, Mary. She is heavy with child and needs a place to rest. Surely you must have some small corner for her. You would not turn her away, would you? She is so tired."

Now, for the first time, the Innkeeper relaxed his stiff stance and looked down at Mary. With that, there was a long pause, long enough to make the audience a bit tense with embarrassment.

"No! Begone!" the prompter whispered from the wings.

"No!" Wally repeated automatically. "Begone!"

Joseph sadly placed his arm around Mary, Mary laid her head upon her husband's shoulder, and the two of them started to move away. The Innkeeper did not return inside his inn, however. Wally stood there in the doorway, watching the forlorn couple. His mouth was open, his brow creased with concern, his eyes filling unmistakably with tears.

And suddenly this Christmas pageant became different from all others.

"Don't go, Joseph," Wally called out. "Bring Mary back." And Wallace Purling's face grew into a bright smile. "You can have my room."

Some people in town thought that the pageant had been ruined. Yet there were others—many, many others—who considered it the most Christmas of all Christmas pageants they had ever seen.

Room in My Heart

*We desire to be able to welcome Jesus
at Christmastime, not in a cold manger...
but in a heart full of love and humility,
in a heart so pure, so warm
with love for one another.*

MOTHER TERESA

An Unusual Year

BY CHRISTIAN DORNBIERER

During May one year our first shipment of poinsettia starter shoots was delivered to our greenhouse. As I helped unload the flats, I wondered if I had ordered more than my customers would need.

I finally managed to submerge that concern with faith in God's guidance. He had led Margaret and me into this work when we had nothing. After several years' struggle we finally had developed our own wholesale flower business. Margaret, our two children, and I all loved working with plants. And the flowers used to celebrate the Christian holidays, especially the poinsettias, gave us the most joy.

Poinsettias are sensitive tropical plants that need love and nurturing. The problem lies in growing the right amount, for they are in demand only a few weeks each year. Grow too few and you have disappointed florists who can't satisfy their customers. Too many and you find that poinsettias, as beautiful as they are, do not make good eating. So we depend on intuition.

We began nurturing the fragile four-inch-high sprigs by repotting them in sterilized soil. Then, keeping them at 70 degrees and misting them regularly, we watched them grow into bushy mother plants. In about a month we took cuttings from each plant.

If we were fortunate, they'd take root and become mother plants themselves. As we repeated the process, the poinsettias began to move across the greenhouse racks like a vast green carpet.

Summer cooled into fall and now, as November clouds scurried above, we knew we must make our final decision. Did we have enough plants to satisfy our customers? An inner guidance told me we needed more. From a local grower I ordered a load of a thousand plants. They looked so nice I ordered a thousand more. A few days later he phoned and offered me a third load at an attractive price. On impulse I told him to send them on.

We moved plants to make room. Then I began to worry. One load would be enough. Two was stretching our luck. But three?

I fought those fears by keeping busy. Now we had to be very watchful. The poinsettias would soon bloom as the top leaves, called bracts, slowly turned red. It's vital that they reach full bloom at Christmas. So we control their development by lowering the temperature to hold them back, or raising it to develop them faster.

Then it happened. Out in the greenhouse one morning, a winter's sun warmed my neck as I breathed in the rich, heady fragrance.

"Chris!" It was Margaret; she had a strange expression on her face. "The phone."

I walked to the phone. On the line was a large Southern grower.

"Your shipment of poinsettias should reach you in a few hours," he said. "Will someone be there?"

I stared dumbly into the phone. Suddenly it all rushed back. Last spring I had decided to try this man's stock and placed a sizable order over the phone. I had completely forgotten it!

Sweat beaded on my forehead. "No! No!" I wanted to shout. "I already have too many!" A battle raged within me. I had a legal right to refuse them. I hadn't signed anything. But I had given my word.

The huge trailer truck strained into our little driveway. By more squeezing and reorganizing, we finally found room. I signed the slip, the truck thundered off, and Margaret and I stood looking at all the poinsettias.

What had I done? I remembered something from the Bible about how a man must keep a promise even if it ruins him. My forgetfulness now threatened to wash out all our work. Panic welled within me.

A leaf brushed my hand. I looked down at it. A blush of crimson was on the leaf. And I thought of the legend of this flower—how a poor Mexican boy on his way to a shrine of the nativity had no gift to offer the Christ child, nothing but a graceful weed he had found in the forest. But as he placed his gift before the altar with all his love, the top leaves miraculously turned flame red, making it a dazzling flower.

These were His flowers, each one a reminder of His presence.

"Margaret," I said, "we'd better raise the temperature for this batch if they're going to bloom in time."

Two weeks passed and then it was time for florists to phone in their orders. They came in the usual trickle at first. Joe, who always seemed to call early, asked for his usual hundred.

Then, as Christmas shopping picked up, more orders came in. Joe phoned for another load. Now repeat orders began to flow in from everywhere.

It turned out to be an unusual year for poinsettias.

By Christmas Eve our greenhouse was bare. Aching in delicious fatigue, I walked into our living room and slumped into a chair by the Christmas tree to dream into its lights—and to thank God again for His Son who taught us to have faith and to remember that "a man's heart plans his way, but the Lord directs his steps."

A Christmas Prayer

Heavenly Father, thank you for the extraordinary
goodness behind all of Your plans for us.
Thank You for the way You direct us, delight us,
and show Your love where we least expect it.
Your goodness came to us, wrapped up in Jesus.
Thank You for the gift of Your Son.

On the Way to Christmas

BY MALA POWERS

In a crowded store one afternoon before Christmas, I watched as the salesclerk grew more and more harassed. Finally she turned to me and with a gasp of irritation said, "Christmas! Who needs it?"

"I do," I said softly. "You and I both need Christmas." She stopped, and I could tell that for a few fleeting seconds she was thinking about that other Christmas, the one that is far removed from the noise of holiday shoppers. She relaxed.

"It's nice to see somebody happy in the middle of all this," she said, and smiled.

That salesclerk was right; I was happy. Maybe I had just been lucky, but years before, I had been led into a highly meaningful season that I'd known very little about—Advent.

It happened when my son, Toren, was a small child. As an actress with a busy schedule outside the home, I was determined, as a good mother, to bring up Toren with a love for the Lord. I wanted the holidays to mean more to him than jolly Saint Nick and gifts under the tree; but this was not easy to accomplish. There was too much competition from stores and

26

television, from bags full of toys and red-nosed reindeer. From the start, I'd told Toren about the nativity and baby Jesus, but if you asked him what Christmas meant to him, he always said, "Santa Claus!"

I wasn't against old Santa, but I wanted Jesus to come first.

Then one day a friend gave me the gift that changed both my Christmas and Toren's. It was an Advent calendar, something I'd never seen before, a large, decorative card with little window flaps that opened to reveal pictures underneath, one for each of the twenty-four days of Advent. Each night after that I watched Toren as he opened another window disclosing stars, shepherds, donkeys, then Joseph and Mary, and finally, on the last night, the Christ child. Each time he opened a new one, I'd talk to him about the significance of the picture, and gradually found myself weaving little stories around them. Toren was delighted.

And I was curious. What was the real meaning of Advent, anyway? I knew dimly that it was the season of preparation, that it always included the four Sundays before Christmas. Now I started doing some research and found that the word itself came from the Latin *adventus* and meant the "coming" or the "coming in"; that among the earliest Christians Advent had been a time of fasting and prayer; that during this season in the Middle Ages many of the beautiful rituals had sprung up: the nativity plays and processions of Wise Men, the crèche scenes, the story-telling. I also found that there were Advent wreaths available today, evergreens with four candles apiece, one for each week.

At the end of November the next year I got ready to celebrate my own version of Advent. When the first Sunday evening arrived, we turned down the lights, and with careful ceremony, Toren helped me light the first red candle on our wreath.

"Think of it, Toren," I said quietly. "For centuries and centuries the world was in a kind of darkness, and then God brought to earth a new and beautiful light for everyone: His own Son."

Toren understood. "That was the baby Jesus," he said in an awed whisper.

Each night in the weeks that followed, we'd open another window in our Advent calendar, and I'd find a new story to tell; "The Night the Chimes Rang" or "The Animals' Christmas Eve" or Toren's favorite about the little girl whose parents were too poor to buy her a present, but who in full faith put her wooden shoes by the hearth, and the next morning found the gift of a shivering baby bird inside one of them.

On the second Sunday of Advent, we lit the second candle and I talked about the meaning of the evergreen, how it stood for the eternalness of God and how the circle of the wreath symbolized His all-encompassing love for us.

Gradually, some of Toren's little friends began to come by for our nightly ritual, and before Christmas arrived that year we found that we had created our own neighborhood tradition. It's a custom that continues today, even though Toren is grown now and away from home.

The form of our little Advent observances hasn't changed much over the years. I've had to learn a lot of different stories. We've added prayers to the story-telling. And, actress that I am, I've found ways to heighten the drama of the occasion by such things as ringing a bell to attract the children's attention and bring them to a reverent hush. There aren't as many children in our neighborhood as there used to be, and sometimes there are more grown-ups in my living room than youngsters. But no matter what age, there's a meaning in the Christmas story for everyone.

Any night that I'm at home before Christmas these days, we still try to create, in fifteen minutes or so, a mood of awe and devotion into which Christ can enter. The children in the room learn more about the meaning of His coming, and the adults, including me, seem to derive an added benefit. I think that benefit comes partly from those few minutes of tranquility when, during the most hectic days of the year, we force ourselves to be quiet and let His Being sink into our souls. It's a quietness that I seem to take with me throughout the following day. It's a calm that often I've been able to share with others, even harried salesclerks who suddenly think, if ever so briefly, of the real Christmas, the one that began in the stillness of a night long, long ago.

Joy to the World

*Let this Christmas season be
a renewing of the mind of Christ
in our thinking,
and a cleansing of our lives
by His pure presence.
Let His joy come to our weary world
through us.*

GERALD KENNEDY

Firstborn

BY LINDA CHING SLEDGE

D on't worry," my smiling obstetrician told me. "You're just feeling the third trimester blues. By Christmas you'll be a healthy, happy mommy and won't have time to worry about yourself." But a glance in the mirror on the consultation room wall revealed the blimpiest of them all.

When I stepped into the hall, I knocked over the red and silver MERRY CHRISTMAS sign that stood on a tripod. Outside, the Upper West Side New York streets were icy and gray with piles of sooted snow. I clopped heavily in thick winter boots toward the subway, bending against the wind, wishing I could go home and put my swollen feet into a hot tub. But I had an appointment with the English professor who was advising me about my dissertation. She would be waiting for me. *Some Christmas this will be*, I thought glumly. My first baby, and here I was, six thousand miles away from my family in Hawaii. At twenty-eight. I was still in graduate school and all I had to go "home" to was a small, dark two-and-a-half-room apartment in Queens, an unfinished thesis (about nativity poems in English literature, ironically), a white cat, and a husband who was just as homesick as I.

It wasn't only the discomfort of this last long month that bothered me. I had real doubts about the future. How would I ever finish school with a baby to take care of? Would I have to abandon my dream of a teaching career just when I was so close?

Squeezing between two slim young secretaries in the subway, I rehearsed the excuses I would tell my professor for my unfinished thesis. "I can't meet the December twenty-first due date because I'm having such a difficult pregnancy. I get dizzy spells standing so long in the library stacks." Or "My doctor says there are complications and he advises total bed rest." No, I looked too massively healthy.

I surfaced from underground and merged into the dotted flow of traffic outside the New York Public Library. I crossed wet, slushy 42nd Street and went into the dark mall of the UNIversity building.

Her door was open; I was keeping her waiting...a bad sign. I walked into her office thirty-seven minutes late (she had that sharp European intellectual's insistence on incisive thinking and punctuality). Neat shelves of books rose from floor to ceiling. She sat behind her desk, well dressed in a nicely cut suit, while I tried to shrink inside my green home-sewn parachute. I was convinced that I would be the first pregnant student to flunk out of my program. Several books lay open before her; I could see where passages had been marked in her neat, small handwriting. I dropped my notes into a heap on the rug where they looked at me, as if in reproach for laziness.

"Sorry I'm late," I stammered. "It's just Christmas, you know?" I wasn't sure that she would understand. Could a Jewish person really comprehend the homesickness that Christians feel at Christmastime when they're far from home? Would her exacting professional standards allow for personal doubt and pregnancy paranoia?

Words of lamentation began to pour out of me in a rush. Not the careful excuses I had fabricated on the subway, but the awful truth. How I couldn't concentrate on my work during the last three months. How I missed my parents and couldn't bear facing the holidays and the prospect of giving birth without having them around me. How scared I was to be a mother. How grim, cold, and frightening nativity poems seemed.

I stopped after a while, exhausted. My career, I was sure, was over before it started. I might as well trade in my small library of much-beloved books and battered typewriter for a diaper-changing table. Throughout my speech, my professor was silent, her intent look changing gradually to a softer one. Finally she spoke, not sternly or severely, but with gentleness.

"Well, my dear, academics can't stand in the way of nature, you know. You can always finish a thesis later. But a baby—that is something very, very special." She continued, her eyes shining. "I remember twenty-four years ago when my daughter was born. I worked until the week she came...I had to, there was no maternity leave in those days for untenured professors. She was five months old when I went back...my career complicated my life and hers, but it enriched us both." She stopped, looked at me, and smiled. "My daughter is the most important work I have ever done."

We talked then like mothers.

When I rose to go, she handed me one of the books on her desk.

"I thought this might be useful for your thesis," she said. "You can return it when you're ready to come back. Don't worry about worrying. I worried, You worry, Jesus' mother worried. Hasn't your reading taught you that? After all, Mary was a mother too. All mothers worry...how else should it be when you are opening the door to the universe?"

She hugged me and let me go. Outside on 42nd Street, as busy shoppers jostled me, I glanced at the book in my hand. *Medieval Folk Carols*—it was a subject I had been wrestling unhappily with for the last eight months. The pages fell open to a passage she had carefully marked beforehand. The lyrics leaped before my eyes. It was an ancient English nativity carol that I had studied in her class and forgotten. But now, it seemed, I understood the words fully:

> *A new year, a new year.*
> *A child has been born*
> *To save and to keep us*
> *All who are forlorn,*
> *So blessed be the time!*
> *Blessed be the mother,*

The child also
With benedicamus domino.
So blessed be the time!

Plodding happily down slushy 42nd Street, I thought of Mary's Son and like Mary, I, too, sang.

The Song of Mary

My soul magnifies the Lord,
And my spirit has rejoiced in God my Savior....
For He who is mighty has done great things for me,
And holy is His name.
And His mercy is on those who fear Him
From generation to generation.

LUKE 1:46–50 NKJV

Christmas Found

BY JACQUELINE ZIARKO WERTH

The toy catalogs began arriving in early October. It was then that I began to fear that I was losing my son Matthew to the merchants of Christmas.

He was eight years old and his brother Jonathan—"J.J." we call him—had just turned two. Sometimes J.J. leafed through one or another of the catalogs, but mostly it was Matthew who pored over them, dreaming aloud and making known his wishes and, often, demands. Thumbing through the toy-filled pages, circling the items he wanted, seemed to occupy most of his time.

Since my divorce, I had tried to keep Christmas as close as possible to all the others Matthew remembered: full of hope and wonder and excitement. But as November became December, it was clear that this Christmas wasn't quite making it. The outward signs were there all right. We had the tree up early, a wreath hanging on the front door.

But Matthew seemed hypnotized by the catalogs. Every day, after school and homework, they'd be lugged out to the kitchen table and the monotonous "I want, I want" would begin. It was like a chant that grew louder and more forceful with every toy added to the list.

At first I paid little attention to it. Then one afternoon the intensity of his desire for "things" started to get to me. What kind of a child was I raising? Was he so wrapped up in his own wants that he missed the real meaning of Christmas?

The next day I went through the bookshelf and pulled out a children's nativity book. When Matthew got home from school, we sat down with J.J. between us and read about the most important birthday in the history of man.

When we finished reading the story, I closed the book feeling satisfied that I had reminded Matthew where the true meaning of Christmas really lay: in a manger in Bethlehem, not in outer-space action figures and electronic games.

The next afternoon, he was back at the catalogs again.

I lost my temper. "Matthew, didn't we sit down yesterday and read all about baby Jesus and how He had nothing more than a wooden crib full of hay to sleep on? You're old enough to know that Christmas isn't all Santa Claus and new toys. It's a lot, lot more. Now go upstairs and clean up your room!"

As Christmas approached, I became even more depressed. I knew Matthew had heard what I said, but the impact wasn't there. My child, my Christian child who went to church every Sunday, didn't care about the priorities of Christmas.

The day before Christmas arrived, early in the afternoon, my ex-husband came, laden with gifts. We had agreed to spend Christmas Eve together for the children's sake. But as soon as Mark walked in the door he announced that the visit would be briefer than expected. "There's a blizzard warning in effect and the tollway is starting to ice up already. I hate to do this, but fifty miles is a long drive in weather like this."

The boys seemed happy with even the small amount of time their father could spend with them. Then Mark left and the cold, cloudy day dripped into evening, Christmas Eve. We dressed for church and I went to make a few phone calls to see who could share the evening with us, now that our plans had been changed. But I hung up the receiver without ever dialing. *Don't be foolish, everyone has plans for Christmas Eve, I said to myself. We'll just spend the evening together.*

During the church service, J.J. fell asleep on my lap and Matthew squirmed in his seat next to me. Afterward we went up to the manger scene with its full-size figures and fragrant hay. Kneeling in front of it, J.J. still dozing on my shoulder, I heard people greeting one another in cheerful voices. Some were families I knew, but at this moment I felt far apart from them. I gazed at the faces of Mary, Joseph, and the Christ child, thinking, *This is the festival of the Holy Family...have we somehow become strangers to them too?*

In the parking lot, the drizzle had changed to snow. By now J.J. was awake and crabby from falling asleep at an odd time. He sat in the car whining as Matthew tried to soothe him by telling him it was only a matter of time before Santa delivered the toys.

Santa, Santa!

As I stood wiping slushy snow off the windshield, the tears wanted to come so bad. But I just wouldn't let them. Not on Christmas Eve.

At home I got the boys ready for bed, and then they climbed into my lap to hear "'Twas the Night before Christmas," part of our ritual ever since Matthew was born. The words, memorized from so many years of reading, sounded mechanical. The way I felt.

I settled J.J. easily into his crib. In Matthew's room I found him already under the covers but wide awake. I kissed him. "Try to fall asleep now." He closed his eyes tightly and I turned off the light.

Downstairs I made a pot of tea and sat down in front of the fireplace, adorned with the empty stockings. There should have been a crèche on the mantel. There should have been so many things about this Christmas.

I looked around the room and tried to find something, anything, that would make me feel the Christmas spirit. My eyes settled on the lighted tree, then on the snow falling on the evergreens outside the front window, making a picture-perfect scene. But it seemed cold and lifeless. I was so lonely.

The tea grew cold. I was just getting up to take the tray into the kitchen and start bringing the gifts from their hiding place when I heard his voice: "Mom?"

I was so startled that I lost my balance and sat back down in the chair.

"I couldn't sleep, Mom."

"Matthew, you must go back to bed."

"Mom!"

"Yes, what is it?" I asked.

"I know there isn't any Santa Claus. I know you're Santa Claus." He jumped off the last step and came over to me, climbing onto the chair as he always did, still so easily, still so little-boyish, I put my arms around him.

"What makes you think so?"

"Oh, I heard some of the older kids talking. I kind of thought that was the way it was, but I wasn't really sure. I didn't know if I should tell you, so I just went along with it like always."

Suddenly my little eight-year-old had crossed one of the borders of childhood!

"Let's roast some marshmallows," I said abruptly, eagerly. "Want to?"

He nodded. "But first, one thing," he said, turning around to me and getting off my lap. "Can I help you make Christmas for J.J.?"

"Of course," I said.

"Great!" Matthew said, already taking command. "Let's get the crèche for the mantelpiece. J.J.'s got to know for sure that most of all Christmas is Jesus."

It was then I knew Christmas had arrived. And I was the one who'd been worried about all those toy catalogs! How good it felt, suddenly, to be a mother. To know that all the little efforts

I'd made to show the boys the real meaning of Christmas hadn't been for nothing.

We walked out into the breezeway that connected the garage to the house and lifted the crèche out of its box.

Overhead, in the holy night, we heard the bells of St. Linus Church begin to ring out "The First Noel," announcing the hour of the ancient, infinite miracle.

The All of Christmas

God grant you the light in Christmas, which is faith;
the warmth of Christmas, which is love;
the radiance of Christmas, which is purity;
the righteousness of Christmas, which is justice;
the belief in Christmas, which is truth;
the all of Christmas, which is Christ.

WILDA ENGLISH

Ten Precious Minutes

BY NELSON SOUSA

A week before Christmas, my partner, Ray, and I were working as construction divers at a bridge site near Somers Point, New Jersey. Snow had begun to fall early, and by noon it had gotten so heavy we had to knock off work.

As we waded through parking-lot drifts, I noticed that my boss, John, was driving a car without snow tires.

"Hey John," I said to him, "why don't you let me drive you home? I don't think you'll make it with those tires."

John considered for a moment, then nodded. "Okay, Nelson, you might be right." But as he started toward my pickup, he stopped and turned back to his car. "Oh, I almost forgot," he said, reaching into its trunk. "Here's your spare dry suit I borrowed last month. I finally remembered to bring it back."

I was about to take the suit to our onsite trailer office where we store gear. But since it had some holes in it, I decided to take it home to repair. I threw it into the back of my pickup. It was the first time in my ten years of diving that I had traveled anywhere with one of these protective rubber suits. They were always stored at work.

John, Ray, and I piled into my truck. The drive north through the snow was rough, stop-and-go all the way. What should have taken us one hour took over three. But we spent the time talking about Christmas and the toys we were buying our kids.

I didn't really mind going out of the way for John, but by the time we got to his turnoff it was past three o'clock. We turned into his street. A fire engine roared by and stopped at the end of the block. There was a big commotion down there.

"Oh dear God, no...," John said. Ahead was an alarming tableau: a frozen pond, an ominous black hole in its center. Fire trucks with lights flashing and people crowding the bank. A woman squalling and weeping.

"Somebody must have fallen through the ice," Ray said.

I pulled the pickup over to the side, jumped out, grabbed my dry suit from the back, pulled it on, and ran to the pond. Ray stumbled along behind me zipping me up.

A grim-faced firefighter told us that a six-year-old boy had walked out on the ice and fallen in. "But it's hopeless," he groaned. "The ice is too thin for us to get out there." Two men had already tried. Even a ladder laid on the ice didn't work. And the water was so cold that anyone falling into it would be shocked into unconsciousness in minutes.

"I'll try," I said. Someone tied a rope around my waist and I headed out, splintering the ice into shards as I beat my way through it. By the time I reached the hole where the boy had disappeared, my hands were bleeding from the exertion.

Icy water surged through the holes in the suit I was going to repair. I knew I had only a minute or two for a dive. Then I discovered I had left my heavy diver's belt back at the job. Without it to weight me down, it would be hard to swim underwater in my buoyant rubber suit. But I had to get down to the bottom.

All I could do was force my body down. The water looked black. About six feet down I touched the bottom, then bobbed up like a cork. Up and down, up and down I plunged, working partway around the opening in the ice frantically feeling for a body. But there was nothing, only frigid water and a slick muddy bottom. Where was he?

Gasping, coughing from exhaustion, I cried out in desperation: "He's not here! I can't find him. Where is he?"

Looking up across the pond, I saw a tall blond man in a light jacket standing by himself in the snow. He raised his arm and pointed to a spot on the side of the hole opposite me.

I pushed to the spot and thrust myself down. The ice-cold water closed over my head, and then my foot touched something. The boy's body! I surged up again. Now, with violent arm movements, I forced myself down and wrapped my feet around the body and drew it up. Floating on my back, I pulled the limp, sodden form across my chest and held him tight.

The little boy's soaked blue jacket seemed glued to him. I pulled back the hood covering his head and screamed. The pinched face was as blue as the jacket. He was not breathing. I could not look at him anymore.

"Pull me back!" I yelled, and the rope tightened around me as firefighters heaved on it, hauling me to the bank. John jumped into the water, took the form, and passed it to waiting medics. I staggered upright, untied the rope, and headed toward them when two policemen grabbed me. "C'mon," one urged, "get into our squad car and warm up."

"But the boy...!" I yelled. By now the ambulance's doors had slammed shut and it sped away, siren wailing. I stood shaking my head, feeling helpless, wishing I could have saved him.

John, my boss, took me to his house where I warmed up some more and then Ray and I drove home. When I walked in, my wife, Patricia, was preparing dinner. I didn't even kiss her, just stumbled over to the sofa and slumped down sobbing. It had all been so useless.

Pat looked at Ray. "Nelson pulled a little boy out of the pond," Ray explained.

Patricia had cooked my favorite dish, beef stroganoff, but I couldn't touch it. I could only sit on the living-room sofa thinking about that poor little fellow and how his parents were feeling.

Patricia called the hospital where the boy had been taken. They told her that little Michael Polukard had been underwater for around ten minutes. He was unconscious, in serious condition. A priest had given him last rites, but he was alive.

What a Christmas, I thought, staring into the glowing lights on our tree. Under it was our nativity scene; the manger bed was empty—our custom is to place the baby Jesus in it on Christmas

Eve. I felt even worse thinking about a real little bed that was empty that night.

I looked gloomily around the room. On the TV set stood two white angels Patricia had made for the house that year. One held a string of stars, the other played a harp. How frivolous it all seemed now. Angels! I remembered how my Portuguese grandmother used to tell us kids about the angels who sang of Jesus' birth to the shepherds that long-ago night. But that night angels and Jesus didn't seem very real to me. And yet, my heart grieved so for the little boy that I did the only thing left for me to do. I leaned my head down and prayed for him. I asked God to help him live.

Hours passed as I sat, moodily staring at the wall. Patricia put our two little girls to bed and Ray tried to encourage me. "He's still alive, you know," Ray said. "There's hope. You should just be grateful that you knew where to find him in that pond."

I looked up. "I didn't know where he was, Ray," I said. "It was that big blond guy who pointed me to the right spot. If it hadn't been for him, I never would have found the boy."

Ray looked puzzled. "That's the strangest thing, Nelson. You keep talking about some guy on the other side of the pond but" —he scratched his head—"there wasn't anybody over there."

About nine o'clock the phone rang. Patricia took it, then handed it to me. "It's Michael's father. He wants to thank you."

With shaking hand, I took the phone. "Don't worry about me," I blurted, "all I want to know is how your little boy is."

Stan Polukard said Michael was still in serious condition, but it looked as though he was going to make it. The very coldness of the water had slowed Michael's body functions, he explained, reducing his need for oxygen. I gave a big sigh of relief and, in my heart, thanked God for saving the little boy. Then I was able to fall into bed and sleep.

We kept in close touch with the hospital the following days, but the news wasn't good. The Polukards had been warned that Michael might have extensive brain damage. The doctors worried about all the time that had passed before his heart and lungs had resumed functioning. A test of his brain by an electroencephalogram had shown "inconclusive" results. Doctors said that only after he regained consciousness would they know how much he'd been damaged.

We learned that his mother and father had moved into the hospital to stay with the boy. The news reported that they were praying for him around the clock. People everywhere sent encouraging messages, saying they were praying with them. I didn't know that there were that many strong believers.

The papers kept up a running account of Michael's plight. Eileen and Stan Polukard continued to talk to their little boy, who lay unconscious, connected to a respirator, a heart monitor, and intravenous lines. The doctors tried to protect them from false hope.

"Remember," one doctor warned Eileen, "the child you knew may no longer exist."

On the third day, Friday, the medical staff took Michael off the respirator. Stan and Eileen continued their patient, prayerful vigil at their son's bedside. Suddenly Michael began to stir. Then, opening his eyes, he slowly turned toward them. "Hi Mom, hi Dad," he whispered.

On Monday afternoon, Christmas Eve, we got a phone call.

"Michael's home!" my wife shouted. The Polukards had called saying that tests showed Michael completely well and normal and that they could take him home. They invited us to their house to celebrate with them.

Patricia and I bundled our two little girls into the car and hurried over.

Michael was dressed in pajamas and sitting on the living-room sofa when we came in. "Do you know who I am?" I asked. For the rest of the evening he wouldn't leave my side. And as we talked he happened to mention that one of the first things he saw when he opened his eyes in the hospital was an angel.

"An angel?" I said, surprised.

There had been an angel there, all right. A big paper angel had hung over Michael's bed as part of the hospital's Christmas decorations.

Angels again. Once more I thought of that mysterious time my grandmother used to tell us about when the angels spoke to the shepherds in the fields and told them about the little baby lying in a manger.

I pictured our own little crèche in our living room at home. When we'd get back, our two little girls would place the baby Jesus in His manger bed.

I glanced up and saw Michael in his father's arms and I gave thanks to the One who had sent us His Son...and who, I now knew for certain, sent His help, somehow, someway, so that another little bed would be warm tonight.

But there was another picture in my mind, a tall blond man standing alone in the snow beside the pond, pointing. Who was he? In all the weeks and months to come, I would find no one who had seen him there. On this happy Christmas Eve, in a room filled with quiet celebration, I couldn't help but wonder.

Christmas Wonder

God's loving initiative to step into time and space to restore us to Himself is still a cause for wonder and praise.

The Stocking

BY JIM HINCH

A shriek of frustration came from the dining room. I poked my head in from the kitchen, where I was drying dishes. The table was cluttered with wrapping paper, boxes, ribbons, bows, scissors, felt, thread, buttons, and a sewing machine. Half draped across the sewing machine was a red felt Christmas stocking. It looked like my wife, Kate, had just thrown the stocking. "It's ruined!" she cried.

"What?" I asked.

"That." She jabbed a finger at the stocking. "There are moth holes in the back. How could I not have noticed? Now Frances won't have a stocking!"

Kate had been working on it for weeks. "My brothers and sister and I all had handmade stockings," she'd explained. "So I have to sew Frances a stocking." Frances was our one-year-old daughter, at that moment asleep in her crib. It didn't matter that Christmas is one of the busiest seasons for Kate, a priest at an Episcopal church. It didn't matter that she'd had to trek all over Manhattan to finally find a tiny fabric store in Chinatown with the kind of wool she felt she needed. It especially didn't matter that I'd pointed out Frances was too young to care about stockings, or

50

that I'd pleaded for a peaceful, stress-free Christmas. "You could try being more supportive," she'd replied.

Now Christmas was just days away. Soon my mom, her friend, and my brother would be arriving to stay with us. Kate had to write a sermon. Gifts were waiting to be wrapped. And there was the stocking. Kate picked it up and ran her finger over the holes. "The felt must have been old," she said. She'd already sewn ribbon across the top. Flower-shaped buttons and gold thread to write Frances's name lay on the table. "I don't know if I have time to start over." She looked at me. "Frances needs a stocking!"

"Well," I said, "I tried to tell you—"

Her face hardened. "Jim, I don't need a Christmas lecture right now. If you're not going to help, let me figure it out."

She turned back to the stocking. I retreated to the kitchen. The counter was cluttered there too. Kate was baking sugar cookies to give to her colleagues. One batch cooled on a rack. Powdered sugar spilled from a bowl. The oven timer ticked down. Gift bags of chocolate from parishioners lined up next to presents for Frances, some from people I didn't even know. The timer beeped. "Could you take those cookies out?" Kate called. I set down the dishtowel. *I don't even like sugar cookies*, I thought.

This wasn't the first time Kate and I had disagreed about Christmas. I remembered airily telling her roommate when we were dating how foolish I thought it was for couples to argue over such a thing. "What's to argue about? It's just a holiday." Well, the next year I did have a few objections. Why did Kate insist on getting a tree when we weren't even going to be home? We were spending that Christmas with family on the West Coast. Didn't she know some of those ornaments she'd saved all those years were kind of tacky? I came home from work one day to hear Bing Crosby on the stereo. Bing Crosby's not really my style. And this business of making cookies for everyone at church—what a hassle! Add to that hours of gift-wrapping and exhausting Christmas services. I felt like some sort of Christmas machine was taking over our lives.

Actually, there was more to it than that. I have a vexed relationship with Christmas. I'm not sure why. My own holiday memories are wonderful. I'd lie awake late into the night at my grandmother's house, my brother in the next bed, both of us straining to hear the slightest rustle of Santa's arrival. We competed over who got to hang the final angel ornament on the Christmas tree Advent calendar. We got to open one gift on Christmas Eve, a moment of exquisite, torturous deliberation. We ate roast beef and lots of pie.

Somehow, though, by the time I was grown up, I'd decided Christmas was one of my least favorite holidays. I love the church season of Advent. I love Christmas Eve services with all their candles and ancient carols. And I love especially the idea of setting time aside to remember that moment two thousand years ago when everything changed. I'm overcome staring at the slightly beat-up, out-of-scale crèche our church erects before the altar. I try to reconcile the enormity of the event with the tiny helplessness of the baby. Some vast mystery of God is expressed in that helplessness. What is it?

The rest of Christmas, though, I can do without. All the gift-giving feels like consumerism run amok. The cheer seems forced. People exhaust themselves lugging packages and fractious kids across the country. Where's God in that?

I took the cookies from the oven and set them on the cooling rack. Why did that stocking matter so much to Kate? Why, for that matter, were we arguing so much more this year? I'd made my peace with the Christmas ornaments. And I thought we'd solved the Bing Crosby problem—Kate played him when I wasn't around. Somehow, though, Frances's arrival seemed to have ratcheted up the holiday tension. I dried the last of the dishes and decided to leave Kate alone. If she wanted to let the Christmas machine whip her into a frenzy, fine.

We got ready for bed, brushing our teeth in silence. I wandered into the living room and looked to where my old stocking—made by a friend of my parents'—and Kate's hung, softly lit by Christmas tree lights. Kate's was pretty cute, I had to admit, with KATIE sewn in felt letters and a little jingle bell on the toe. I tried to picture her all those years ago holding the stocking in her tiny hands. What would Frances look like holding hers?

We got into bed. Kate lay quietly, hands folded across her chest. I pretended to read. "I'm not going to make the stocking," she said quietly. I put down my book. "I'd have to start from scratch and I don't have time. I still have to write a sermon and wrap up those cookies."

I was about to find a delicate way to say, "Told you so," when I looked over and saw her tears. I took her hand. "Kate, what's wrong?" She didn't answer. "What's wrong? Tell me."

She was silent awhile longer, then suddenly it all came out in a rush. "I'm a terrible mom and Frances is going to have the worst Christmas. I know you say she won't know, but I'll know. My mom always did so many great things for us at Christmas. She and Dad used to set up our little crèche, and late Christmas Eve night they'd put the baby Jesus in there and I always thought He appeared by magic. Now we're so far away from them and you don't even care about Christmas. How do I make all that happen for Frances by myself? If I was a better mom I could do it, but I can't."

She wiped her eyes. All my ranting about Christmas, my tsk-ing about to-do lists—it shriveled up. I reached over and put my arms around her. "Don't say that," I said. "You're a great mom." We lay like that a long time. I thought about the messy dining room table, the sugar cookies, the gifts. And I thought about the stocking. How on earth could I ever have objected to giving Frances, no matter how old, a taste of beloved Christmas memories? That wasn't the Christmas machine. That was love, as clear an expression of God's vast mystery as anyone could ask for. Besides, it mattered to Kate and Kate mattered to me. I held her tight. And I told her we were all—yes, all of us—going to have a wonderful Christmas.

Christmas Memories

The things we do at Christmas
are touched with a certain extravagance,
as beautiful, in some of its aspects,
as the extravagance of Nature in June.

ROBERT COLLYER

A Christmas House

by Brian Jones

I'm going to tell you about a movie that changed my life. Unexpectedly, to say the least. Until then my favorite films were all about flying, movies like *Top Gun* and *The Right Stuff*. That's because I planned to be a military pilot like my father and then someday an astronaut. The posters on my bedroom walls showed F-4s, the space shuttle, and Han Solo's *Millennium Falcon* from the *Star Wars* movies. But that particular afternoon my mom was chuckling over a movie on TV called *A Christmas Story*. "Come watch this with me," she said. I was thirteen.

I laughed at the boy with the horn-rimmed glasses who wanted a Red Ryder BB gun for Christmas and seemed destined never to get it from Santa or his hapless parents. Everything seemed to go wrong with the Parker family—the faulty furnace in their house, the neighbors' dogs that ate up their turkey dinner, the lights on the Christmas tree that blew the fuse. And yet, everything was right with them too—their affection for each other, their warmth, their forgiveness, and their sweet trust that, despite any of the disappointments of life, things would turn out all right for them.

A Christmas Story became an annual ritual for our family. Mom, Dad, my sister Jennifer, and I would sit on our couch in sunny California and get a real dose of a wintry Midwestern Christmas. We could repeat snatches of dialogue like a code. Take the lamp. The father wins it in a contest, a leg in a fishnet stocking with a shade on top. When the box arrives, it says THIS END UP, with the *T* missing and FRAGILE on top. "Fra-GEE-lay," the dad says. "It must be Italian." My sister and I could crack each other up with that one mangled word. "It's a major award!" the father announces, and that made us laugh too. The whole movie is incredibly silly, yet it touched something in our family, a quirky kind of joy that drew us closer. A kind of affirmation that no matter how crazy life got, we always had each other.

Flying still consumed my imagination, though. I enrolled in the U.S. Naval Academy at Annapolis, my father's alma mater. Annapolis, because so many of its alumni were astronauts. From there I'd enter flight school and then on to NASA. My dream, though, was about to come crashing to earth.

Once I got to flight school at Naval Air Station Pensacola I had to have a physical exam. In those days you needed near perfect sight. The flight surgeon checked my heart, my blood pressure, my weight, my height (you had to be able to reach the controls). Everything was perfect. Then the ophthalmologist asked me to read the smallest line on the eye chart...several times. "Why don't you try again, son," said the flight surgeon. He wanted me to pass.

"Sir," I said, "I tried three times and I still can't read it."

Devastated. That's how I felt. Just blown away. It was the worst day of my life. I went back to my apartment, gave my roommates the thumbs-down, called up my dad, and then flopped on the coach. I was in shock. Couldn't even watch TV. It was like something died in me. I've heard people say that our dreams come from God. Well, at age twenty-two I wondered why God would give me so much disappointment.

I bounced around, ended up going into navy intelligence, but I never had the passion for it like I did for flying. I'd been at it for a couple months when I came home to find a huge crate at my apartment, sent by FedEx. In intelligence training we'd been warned not to open anything that looked too weird, but something about this box was strangely familiar. FRAGILE, it said in block lettering, THIS END UP.

Like the dad in *A Christmas Story*, I had to use all my strength to pry the huge thing open. I took off the top and dug inside. Out came a plastic leg draped in a fishnet stocking. The lamp from the movie! I laughed till I cried. It was the funniest thing I'd ever seen, and my first real moment of joy since flunking the eye exam.

"It's a major award for dealing with life's disappointments," my dad said on the phone, laughing. My parents had made it themselves, buying the mannequin leg in the garment district in LA, gluing some fringe on the lampshade, finding fishnet stockings at a ballet shop. Its warm glow reminded me that things would turn out all right like they did for the boy in the movie. God had other dreams in store for me. I just had to trust. And laugh a little.

Good things did happen. I got married to a wonderful woman I met in the navy. Beverly was in intelligence too, but her career took her on long stints onboard ship while I worked on base. Shortly after our marriage I told her I was thinking about getting out of the service. We talked a lot about possible careers for me. "Maybe I'll take a job-training program in retail or marketing," I e-mailed her one day. But then, sitting at my computer, I had a brainstorm: I'll make leg lamps. Crazy, right? Still, the leg lamp cheered me up. Maybe it could others too.

I checked out mannequin legs at Victoria's Secret (with Beverly's help!) and found a way to order them. I got a supplier for lampshades, fishnet stockings, high heels, everything I needed (the suppliers must have thought I was into something pretty weird). I assembled the lamps and took orders through a website, a couple a week at first, but they kept coming...and coming. I quit the navy and went into business for myself. By my second Christmas, I was selling two thousand lamps a year. Yep. You heard right. Two thousand fishnet-stockinged leg lamps annually.

Poor Beverly. Just imagine her trying to explain what her new husband did for a living! Everybody onboard teased her— but they also bought my lamps! Even the commanding officer. One winter they were at sea when the CO noticed that the old Cleveland, Ohio, house used in the movie *A Christmas Story* was up for sale on eBay. He sent the listing to Beverly. "Thought this would amuse you," he wrote.

She e-mailed me: "BTW, the CO told me that the house they used in the movie with the leg lamp is for sale on eBay. LOL."

I didn't LOL. I got right on eBay, contacted the owner, and wrote, "Hey, I'd like to buy your house." In less than twenty-four hours we cut a deal.

I suppose you could say it was an impulse purchase. Something as crazy as what might have happened in the movie. I knew exactly what that house looked like. I could see the lace curtains at the window and the staircase where Ralphie stood, humiliated in his pink bunny suit. I could picture the old cast-iron sink and hear the furnace rattling. It wasn't just a senti-mental idea, you see. Having sold thousands of leg lamps, I knew how many other people were out there, obsessed with this gentle movie and its funny family. There had to be something in that. I e-mailed Beverly: "The Parkers' house is mine."

"Are you serious????" she quickly e-mailed back.

"Yes!!! I bought it."

Her next e-mail was just one line: "I don't know whether to laugh or to cry."

I e-mailed back: "It's a major award!" By then we were both laughing.

So I redid the interior to look exactly like the movie. Same wallpaper, same fixtures, all the same furniture.

Last year, right after Thanksgiving, I opened the house up to visitors, seven dollars for adults. That first weekend we had over 4,500 guests, and they kept coming, no matter what the season! We opened a museum and gift shop across the street, and sell all sorts of souvenirs, including *A Christmas Story* Monopoly game, and, of course, more leg lamps. It's brought a lot of business to the area, which people are grateful for.

Today I often think about who I was when I first saw that movie and what my big dreams were then. I didn't become a jet pilot or an astronaut, but the new dream God gave me has made me happier than I ever could have imagined. I love this little business. I love the way it makes people happy. I love listening to the comments visitors make when they come through the house, especially families.

If anyone asks, I can tell them that lots of good things still happen to you after you've gotten the biggest disappointment of your life. But then they probably know that already. They've all seen that little, funny, charming, oddly life-changing movie, the movie that changed me.

Share the Joy

For somehow, not only at Christmas,
but all the long year through,
the joy that you give to others
is the joy that comes back to you.

JOHN GREENLEAF WHITTIER

Ugly the Beautiful

BY FAYE ROBERTS

At first it looked as if we weren't going to have a tree at all that Christmas.

In years past, getting the tree had been one of the happiest events for our family. My husband, Chris, and I would bundle our three kids on the back of our snowmobiles and roar up through the crisp, glittering snow to Cedar Mountain to check out at least fifty trees before selecting the one that was "just perfect."

But that was before Chris died and my children and I moved two hundred miles to Montrose. Facing that first bleak Christmas as a young widow, I could hardly bear the thought of getting a tree for the holiday. That's when I thought that perhaps an inexpensive artificial tree would do.

I drove sixty miles to Grand Junction, only to find the shopping mall filled with impatient shoppers. A broken ornament crunched under my shopping cart as I weaved my way to a display of artificial trees. One tree was decorated in red plastic poinsettias, another in white doves. A third was made of a glittery silver substance, and yet another was flocked with "snow" from an aerosol can. A plastic baby Jesus for an outdoor nativity scene was on sale for $19.95. After the manager announced a special on microwave ovens, a distraught woman began arguing with her husband, saying, "We can't afford one," but he grunted that he'd use his credit card and headed toward the housewares. Even plastic money!

I abandoned my half-filled basket, hurried to the exit, and drove the sixty miles back home in angry tears: anger at the couple, anger at the store's plastic Christmas, anger at my husband for dying and leaving me to face Christmas alone, and most of all, anger at God for letting it happen. I resolved there would be no Christmas this year, no presents, no angel cookies, and absolutely no artificial tree. When I arrived home, I took the Christmas cards I had been working on and shoved them into a drawer, slamming it shut.

December was turning out to be an appropriate ending to a terrible year. Chris had died unexpectedly in January when a heart valve ruptured while he was loading a snowmobile. We were both twenty-six. From then on there seemed to be nothing but problems. I struggled with the never-ending red tape of insurance, taxes, and Social Security. Eight-year-old Amy began having problems at school. Five-year-old Mandy couldn't sleep and started sucking her thumb again. And every time Christopher, age four, did something wrong, it was because he missed his daddy. I cut back to part-time work at the bank and became a night owl, sleeping during the day and pacing the floor at night.

In September we packed up and moved to Montrose. The kids settled into the new school. I planted fruit trees and bought a rototiller. I really thought we were coping, until December.

I'd always loved Christmas, the music, the smell of Christmas goodies, watching the kids decorate Christmas cookies, but my favorite ritual was bringing back and putting up the Christmas tree. Of course, the "just perfect" tree would always be too big, so Chris would cut off the bottom and use the extra boughs for wreaths and garlands. The cedar's fragrant berries would fill the house with their spicy smell. I would make popcorn and heat cider while Chris strung the lights. The kids would throw the icicles on in globs while I patiently put them on one strand at a time.

Last Christmas Eve after midnight mass, Chris and I had turned off all the lights in the house and we'd sat staring at the tree, counting our many blessings: the children, our families, our home in the country, and our love of the Lord and His love for us. Now I was in a strange house, in a strange town, and in the strange situation of actually having considered buying an artificial tree. I missed the mountain, home, and Chris more than I ever thought possible.

The yellow school bus stopped out front, and the kids piled into the house, dropping lunch boxes, books, and gloves. As we sat in the kitchen drinking cocoa, I announced, "There will be no Christmas tree this year. The season has become too plastic and phony. It is a time for greedy merchants to bleed people, trying to get them to spend money they don't have. We won't participate in it."

All three voices cried out in unison, "But, Mom, that's not fair!" And three gloomy faces followed me around the house the rest of the week.

On Sunday the kids stayed after church to practice for the Christmas program, and came home full of Christmas spirit. I softened at Christopher's big, sad brown eyes and consented to buy a small tree, as long as it was not fake. Few were left to choose from at the lot by the grocery store. It could be either a tall, spindly pine, or a short, scraggly spruce. We chose the latter. A salesman tied it to the top of the Subaru and we took it home.

The tree wouldn't fit in the stand; the trunk was too fat. I whittled it down with a butcher knife, leaving globs of sticky sap on the carpet. The needles scratched my arms as I tried to set the tree back in the stand. It kept tilting to one side. I got some baling wire from the barn and wired it to the curtain rod. I turned the bare side to the wall, but no matter how I turned it, the tree had a big hole gaping in the middle. The branches drooped pitifully. It was absolutely the worst-looking Christmas tree I had ever seen. Disgusted, I went to the bedroom and left the kids to decorate the tree by themselves.

Later I heard a timid tapping as Mandy's bright blue eyes peeked around the bedroom door. "Mommy, would you come put the angel on the top of the tree?" she asked, barely controlling her enthusiasm.

"Not now, honey. I'm busy folding these clothes."

Her shoulders slumped as she turned to go, then she turned back and asked, "Could you at least come and see, just for a minute?" I felt guilty for taking away her spark of joy and relented.

Amy had strung the lights, forgetting to check for burned-out bulbs. Mandy and Chris had put too many balls on the bottom, leaving the top bare where they could not reach. The kids were so proud of the job they had done. When I put the angel on the top, they all declared how beautiful the tree was.

The neighborhood kids, however, did not see the same beauty and playfully christened the little tree "Ugly." I had to agree with the neighbor kids. The name stuck. Amy would ask Mandy to plug in Ugly's lights. Mandy would ask Chris if he had watered Ugly. Ugly quickly became part of the family.

On Christmas Eve we went to the children's pageant at church. Everyone else seemed to be enjoying the play, but I kept worrying that the boy behind Mandy would scorch her pigtail with his candle as they stood in front of the altar, singing "Silent Night." Gone was that mysterious Christmas wonder and glow that Chris and I had felt at midnight mass the year before. All I felt now was a cold emptiness as I observed husbands and wives holding hands and proudly watching their children.

After punch and cookies, I took the children home and put them to bed, promising to leave the porch light on for Santa. I watched Johnny Carson until I was sure they were asleep, then decided to put off playing Santa until early morning. I flipped off the television.

The soft lights of the Christmas tree flickered in the darkness. As I bent down to unplug them, I noticed a strange present wrapped in paper I had not seen before. On the card was scrawled "To Mommy, Love Mandy" in first-grade handwriting. I smiled and, without thinking, opened the box carefully. There under a layer of pink tissues lay a lamb made of flour-and-salt dough. Next I unwrapped a wise man, his whiskers made from pressing dough through a garlic press. One eye was a little larger than the other; his turban, lopsided. I set him next to the lamb and unwrapped Mary. The hair sticking out from under her blue scarf was the same bright yellow as Mandy's. She had a big red smile on her face. Next came Joseph, and finally baby Jesus sleeping in a manger.

I sat back and admired the family under the flickering lights. The ugly tree held its branches like protective arms over the little family. On the tree was none of the plastic I had been fighting all season, but it was decorated with love and memories: a God's eye made of Popsicle sticks and yarn, a chain of red and green paper strips, a navel orange stuck with cloves, the wooden ornaments my mother had painted for me when I was a small girl, the big white snowflake Chris had made in preschool, and three clip-on glass birds, the only store-bought ornaments Chris and I could afford the first year we were married. Filling the big hole in the middle of the tree was the ornament with a picture of the kids on it.

At that moment it was the most beautiful tree in the world. It stood straight, even though it needed reinforcement.

Just like me! I thought. I too was weather-beaten but was still standing. I had family and friends for my baling wire, my reinforcement. Even though I too felt empty in the middle, I had three terrific kids to help fill the space Chris had left. I had the Lord as my base, and His angels watching over me. I was surrounded with the loving and caring ornaments of memories. Some of my lights had burned out, but others still flickered with the hope of tomorrow.

Seven years have come and gone since I sat beneath that tree on Christmas Eve. I am remarried now and have a four-year-old son, Todd. With my husband, Tom, I have rekindled the tradition of cutting our own tree. When we get it home, it is still too big. But every year, the kids and I remember with pride our Ugly tree. We've had to move our nativity family to a shelf (Todd tried to eat baby Jesus last year), but in my heart it will always belong under the bare branches of the scraggly spruce tree.

The Beauty of the Season

Again Christmas: abiding point of return.
Set apart by its mystery, mood, and magic,
the season seems in a way to stand outside time.
All that is dear, that is lasting, renews
its hold on us: we are home again.

Elizabeth Bowen

Christmas 1914

AUTHOR UNKNOWN

The Great War was only a few months old, but already the two sides were deadlocked in the grisly new pattern of trench warfare. Both the British and Germans had learned to shovel miles-long ditches in the rocky French farmland, ditches from which men blasted at one another with machine guns and mortars. In these muddy, rat-infested trenches, British soldiers opened soggy Christmas greetings from their king while a few hundred yards away German troops read a message from the kaiser.

Between the rows of trenches, where shivering men thought about families at home, lay a barren no-man's-land, a zone of craters and shattered trees where anything that moved was instantly fired at. So narrow was this strip that whenever there was a lull in the roar of the guns, each side could hear the clink of cooking gear from the other.

Late on Christmas Eve, with the sleet tapering off and the temperature dropping, a British Tommy on guard with the Fifth Scottish Rifles heard a different sound drifting across no-man's-land. In the German trenches a man was singing.

"Stille Nacht, heilige Nacht..."

It was a tune the British soldier recognized as "Silent Night, Holy Night." The sentry began to hum along with the melody. Then, louder, he chimed in with the English words, singing an odd duet with his enemy beyond the barbed wire.

"...heilige Nacht..."

"...holy night..."

A second British soldier crawled to the sentry station and joined in. Little by little others on both sides picked up the song, blending their rough voices across the shell-pocked landscape. The Germans broke out with a second carol, "O Tannenbaum," and the British replied with "God Rest You Merry, Gentlemen." On and on the antiphonal singing went. A British soldier with binoculars reported that the Germans had hoisted a ragged evergreen with lighted candles in the branches to the top of the sandbag barrier. As dawn of Christmas day broke, signs appeared on both sides, in two languages: MERRY CHRISTMAS!

Pulled by a force stronger than fear, one by one the soldiers started laying down their arms, creeping beneath barbed wire and around mortar holes into no-man's-land. At first it was just a few men, then more and more, until scores of British and German troops met together in the first light of Christmas day. The boys brought out photographs of mothers and wives, exchanged gifts of candy and cigarettes. Someone produced a soccer ball and the men played on a few yards of crater-free ground.

Then the Soldier's Truce was over.

By mid-morning Christmas day, horrified officers had summoned their men back to the trenches; firing had recommenced. Within hours the Fifth Scottish Rifles issued an order forbidding such contact: "We are here to fight, not to fraternize."

And the soldiers obeyed. The war, as history tragically records, destroyed almost that entire generation of young men on both sides. But there was an indelible memory in the minds of those who lived to recall that first Christmas at the front. The memory of a few hours when their master had been neither king nor kaiser, but the Prince of Peace.

The Prince of Peace

For to us a child is born, to us a son is given,
and the government will be on his shoulders.
And he will be called Wonderful Counselor,
Mighty God, Everlasting Father, Prince of Peace.
Of the greatness of his government
and peace there will be no end.

ISAIAH 9:6–7 NIV

A Christmas Crisis

BY MELVA VANDIVER

I stared out the window at the snow as big flakes covered the two narrow front steps. Always before, I had thrilled at December snowfalls, the perfect backdrop to the carols Dad and I sang as we hung lights on the two spruce trees flanking our door. But not this year. And not that front door. This was the first Christmas since Dad had asked Mom for a divorce.

Mom had taken this small house and moved out, leaving Dad in our old house. She was always the one to be decisive, always at the helm. She'd taken a job when we four kids reached college age and turned each paycheck over to whichever college we attended; she'd haunted rummage and yard sales to clothe us, and stretched chicken casseroles to feed Dad's business associates and our own friends.

Now she was alone, except for me. I, the youngest, had just finished college and was job hunting. In the six months she'd lived in the cramped cracker-box house on this narrow street with one tree per yard, she'd forged ahead with her life. She'd returned to school to complete her degree, taken a part-time job, and joined a support group of divorced women.

But now as Christmas approached, something had changed in her. I'd often find her sitting in the dark, just sitting, staring. Sometimes I'd go to her and sit beside her, and she'd reach for my hand and turn to me and say, "I'm bitter, Melva. I think about Dad with that other woman, and I'm hurt and angry and oh so...lonely."

I too was angry. I never thought I could hate my dad, but I did now. I hated him for what he had done to us. Now with Christmas coming, it all seemed too much.

"Mom, why don't we just forget about Christmas this year?" I asked.

"No, we can't do that," she said. "We'll have Christmas here. I'll invite everybody here—all you children, I mean."

"How?" I asked. "There's not enough room! We can't even open out the dining room table and fit the chairs underneath!"

"We'll just have to eat Christmas dinner off our laps."

"And there'll be Dad rattling around in that big house. I hope he starves! You know he can't boil an egg," I retorted hotly.

We spent the next two weeks like zombies, going through the motions of preparing for a celebration. Each task filled me with more anger. Our tiny tree reminded me of the roomy house I'd lost; one fewer gift to buy symbolized a family unit that existed no more. The same songs and scents that brought pleasure for years now underscored how everything had changed.

On Christmas Eve I dashed into a department store to make a last-minute purchase. I elbowed my way toward a table to find the perfect pair of maroon gloves, but my mind wasn't on the purchase. It was on how angry I felt. My two older sisters had jobs, my brother was married and had a child. They had separate lives. Mom was suffering. And Dad—well, he had removed himself from us.

Now I stood stock still in the middle of the hat-and-glove department while carols rang out over the store's loudspeakers. Christmas was coming and I didn't want to be a part of it. I had never felt more lonely in my life.

When I got home, Mom was humming. She was actually cheerful. The refrigerator was stocked with foods for the next day. There was the cranberry mold, and celery and carrot spikes soaking in water. Olives were chilled, the turkey was thawing, and cornbread-oyster stuffing was piled in a bowl covered with plastic wrap.

"Here, Mel," Mom said, using my childhood nickname and handing me an apron, "help me with the Christmas cookies."

Had something in her spirit changed, or was she just doing a better job of covering up? Not wanting to spoil the moment, I accepted the apron. We cut out the familiar forms of angels, bells, stars, and reindeer, and even joined in snatches of carols. The cookies were in the oven when my brother arrived with his wife and their small son, Joey. We had supper and it was time to leave for the Christmas Eve service. Time was not standing still. Christmas was upon us, ready or not.

The next morning I awoke to the familiar aromas of the Christmas turkey roasting, and of fresh coffee and cinnamon buns, which were Mom's Christmas breakfast treat.

My two older sisters arrived midmorning with packages and suitcases. Mother and I would sleep in the basement and give them our twin beds.

The living room soon became a circus with my nephew, Joey, flinging himself upon his packages, and with our own glee at surprise gifts from one another. I think we all overdid it in an effort to pretend nothing had changed.

We were to the stage of saving bows and wadding up tissue paper when the doorbell rang.

Mom opened the door and there stood Dad.

The room went silent as we gaped at him. "Come in, Richard," Mom said.

Dad entered the room, looking about tentatively, assessing his welcome. I couldn't believe it. Had Mom invited him here? How could she have? How could she?

Joey sailed through this startling moment by tackling Dad's knees. "Hi, Grandpa!"

I turned and fled into the kitchen. I was pretending to check on the turkey a few minutes later when Mom came in and put a hand on my shoulder. I confronted her at once.

"Why?" I demanded.

"Melva," she started, "I wasn't sure that Dad was coming or I would have told you ahead of time."

Quietly she took my hand. "Last night, didn't we pray, 'Forgive us...as we forgive those who have sinned against us'?"

"Mom," I said, trembling, "I can't."

"What's the alternative?" she asked, her voice stronger. "Didn't you see how you and I have been living this month? If we let anger and hurt cut us off, we're isolating ourselves. Then something you said stuck in my head. About Dad rattling about in that big house alone, and how you hoped he starved. I knew we didn't want spiteful thoughts in our heads, especially at Christmas. I wondered if we couldn't set them aside for one day. So I called him."

"But Mom, he could have hung up on you or said hurtful things!"

"I know. That's the chance I took. I had to set aside my pride to do it. I knew I was taking a risk, but I counted on God's Spirit—His Christmas Spirit. And that's what I'm counting on to carry us through the day."

"After the way he's treated you—treated us all!"

"Listen," she said firmly, "we had some good years, your dad and I. To me, you kids are permanent good that came out of those years. There's a lot of life still ahead of us—weddings, graduations, birthdays. I don't want you to have to ask, 'Shall we invite Mother to this, or Dad?' That would separate us all even further. No, Melva, I am going to love your father and you are going to love him. Jesus tells us to love, and no matter what the cost to our pride and vanity, we are going to do it."

She put her arm around me and we went back out.

After we sat down to Christmas dinner, things got easier. As the afternoon passed, Dad even dozed on the sofa while my sisters and I modeled our gifts, and we all tried on a red-brimmed hat, giggling as always. It was tempting to pretend nothing had changed, and painful to remember things had.

I lay on my cot that night and stared into the darkness of the basement, listening to the water pipes and the hum of the furnace. We had made it through Christmas day. Looking back, I'd spent far more energy dreading it than living it.

Future Christmases would be easier now, thanks to Mom. And the feeling of loneliness had gone. With Mom too. Christian love had pushed out the anger inside us.

The Best Gift

How silently,
How silently the wondrous gift is given.
So God imparts to human hearts
The wonders of His heaven.

PHILLIPS BROOKS

Keeping Christmas

BY DOROTHY WALWORTH

Some morning this December I will read an advertisement offering for sale "Christmas novelties." It will leave me cold. An article will doubtless exhort me, "Aren't you tired of wrapping your packages in the same old red and green? Try yellow, for a change." But I like the same old red and green.

An up-to-date Santa Claus in a motorized sleigh is, to me, a monstrosity. I do not wish to hear, on the radio, new strange Christmas music, though it may have the best of contemporary intentions. The old carols are the only music that warms my heart in the December cold. I hope no one will send me a Christmas card with modernistic angels. Nor do I wish to hear the Christmas story except according to the gospel of Saint Luke. Any other version, however brilliant, seems second hand. But when I hear the words, "And there were in the same country shepherds abiding, keeping watch over their flock by night," I become, once again, a humble wondering child. I catch an authentic glimpse of the kingdom of heaven.

When this December comes, I know what I will be doing. It is what I have always done. My family will give me lists of what they want for Christmas. I will give them a list

78

too, but I can never think of anything I want in December, although I can think of plenty all the other months of the year. I will also mark down some names of "People Who Don't Expect Presents," because remembering folks like that gives us all a sort of blissful floating feeling. I will not let myself be depressed when somebody says to me, "Christmas has become commercialized." Nonsense. Christmas is only commercialized for those who let it be that way. Nor will I agree when I hear that feeble weary bromide, "Christmas is only for children." Nonsense again. The more we live, the more Christmas means. Christmas, though forever young, grows old along with us.

I will resolve to economize, and, as usual, be a bit extravagant. I will try to shop early, and be envious of those calm women who announce they have Done Everything by the middle of November. My husband and I will buy wreaths for the front windows of our house. So far we have never been able to afford wreaths for the sides and back. We will go out together and choose our Christmas tree. And just any old tree won't do! We always have our hearts set on a bushy tree, too tall for our living room, which has to be sawed off at the top.

Of course, I will get tired. I will have my secret disappointments too because of wishes on those Christmas lists that I cannot fulfill. Probably I will get a cold. Somewhere in the midst of the rush, I will say to myself, "I just can't seem to feel the Christmas spirit yet this year." And I will get worried chills down my spine for fear the Day might come, and, in my hurry and fatigue, I might not feel the Spirit.

However, just as I worry, the ancient bliss begins to come over me. Little by little I see our ordinary grocery store transformed by festoons of ground pine. All of Main Street becomes rapturously different. My husband calls to me, "There's a carol on the radio," and we listen. Both of us believe there are not enough carols on the radio throughout the Christmas season, and too many crowded, at the end, into a few hours.

The day approaches so near we can say, "next week." Suddenly I am not at all tired. Who could be tired in the midst of a miracle? I scan my lists again, feeling I have not given anyone half enough, and make a final frenzied visit to the stores. My husband is told not to look in the guest room closet, and he warns me not to look under the bed. Our house fills with tissue paper. I am not good at doing up packages; I tie clumsy bows. But who cares? We all hope there will be snow for Christmas, but it really does not matter. As the miracle draws closer, everything else seems small. Nothing can harm the joy of Christmas, when I remember the angel of the Lord's first words to the shepherds were: "Fear not, for behold I bring you good tidings."

The Christmas cards begin to arrive, the cherished record of our friendships. Down from the attic come our Christmas trimmings, which are, in their own way, the story of our married life. They have lasted a long time, because we have been so careful with them. Some ornaments we have had ever since we were married, like the star for the top of the tree. There are the red globes our daughter liked best when she was small, and the horn the kitten almost broke, which was saved in the nick of time. We set on a table our simple crèche, with the figures of the holy family, along with an ox and an ass and the shepherds. We are always sure, each year, the holy child has gotten lost somewhere among all the trimmings, but He is never lost. He lies, as always, in the manger, with the tiny gold light about his head.

On Christmas Eve my husband always has a hard time getting the tree into its metal stand. He pounds and thumps, while I hold on to the trunk. Finally it stands straight. Then we trim the tree with the lights, the ornaments, and, finally, the tinsel. Somehow, in the light from the tree, my husband looks as young as the day we married, and he says I do too. On Christmas Eve, although we may be doing very ordinary things, I feel the same almost unbearable excitement as I did when I was a child. Because something wonderful is about to happen. I cannot help thinking that, at that very moment, the Wise Men are seeing the Star, and there is still no room at the inn.

When the tree is all decorated, I sit down at the piano and my husband and I sing the carols. We do not sound as fine as the radio, but we like it better. Of course, there are voices that used to sing with us, which we can no longer hear. But they seem very close, and there are no tears in our eyes. We like to think our daughter and her husband will arrive on Christmas morning.

And this year, for the first time, they will bring our grandson, nine months old.

We like Christmas Eve best. In the air of expectancy, touched by wonder, we live, for that evening, in the real world, which lies, mysterious, at the heart of life.

But Christmas morning is fine too. First there is going to Church. I am the child of a minister and church is home to me. I have made it part and parcel of my life; I go when I am discouraged, sick, frightened; I go when I am grateful and happy. But church on Christmas morning is special and very holy, for the birth was the beginning of Christianity—the one second chance for the world. And I pray that in the year to come I can be more worthy, and I give thanks for all the year has held since last Christmas, good and bad. I want, before I leave church on Christmas, to look squarely at that "bad" and see it for its worth so I may profit by it in my soul.

After the early church service, we all sit on the floor, beside the tree. We open our presents in turn, each one opening while the others watch. And if our son-in-law tries to open out of turn, our daughter will say firmly, "Remember, on Christmas we do things as we have always done them. There are customs in this house!"

I tell this story because it will happen, not only to us, but to families everywhere, all over this great country, in December. In a world that seems to be not only changing but dissolving, there are tens of millions of us who want Christmas to be the same. With the old greeting, "Merry Christmas," and no other. With the abiding love among people of goodwill that the season brings. We hold fast to our customs and traditions at Christmas, whatever they may be, because they strengthen our family ties, bind us to our friends, make us one with all mankind for whom the child was born.

So, in December, the old cry goes out, "Oh, come, all ye faithful." And we, the faithful, humble in the glory of the Incarnation, do not say that we "spend" Christmas, or "pass" Christmas. We "keep" Christmas: in all the years to come, we must continue, passionately, to keep it. For the Spirit of Christmas is the hope of the world.

Keeping Christmas

How will you your Christmas keep?
Feasting, fasting, or asleep?
...Be it kept with joy or prayer,
Keep of either some to spare;
Whatsoever brings the day,
Do not keep but give away.

ELEANOR FARJEON

A Portion of Thyself

BY ROBERT HALVERSON

When was the last time you read or heard a Christmas story about businessmen that didn't involve commercialism in some way? Think for a minute. Christmas and the Christ child, Christmas and carols, Christmas and angels...yes, of course. But Christmas and businessmen? The words don't seem to belong together, do they?

This thought was hovering in my mind one year when Christmas was approaching with all its warmth and wonder. As a family man, I knew I'd be choosing gifts for four lively kids and a wonderful wife. But what about less fortunate members of the community? The Bible has a lot to say about the importance of helping widows and orphans. What was I doing for them?

I'm a businessman myself, a homebuilder. Somewhere I'd read that the best gift is not something you buy, but something you create yourself. I began to wonder if there might be some way I could donate a portion of my skills as a builder to some person who needed them.

Then a better idea occurred to me. I was vice president of the Home Builders Association here in Lincoln County. What if several of us pooled our skills in such a project? Why couldn't we make that our Christmas gift to the community of Newport?

The more I thought about it, the more excited I became. It would be good for our little town. It would be good for our association, too. Somewhere I had read an article claiming that the public doesn't regard us home-builders too highly; in fact it said that when it came to credibility and trust, we were almost at the bottom of the totem pole, along with used-car salesmen.

That article bothered me a lot. I knew that the thirty-one builders and twenty-nine associates who make up our membership are as warm-hearted and generous a group as you could find anywhere. And I was right, because when I suggested my idea at the November meeting and asked for volunteers, hands shot up all over the room. Before we adjourned, a "Christmas Gift for Lincoln County" committee had been formed.

Our first step was to mail out twenty-one letters to local churches, asking them to help us find a worthy recipient whose home needed to be repaired or restored. We explained carefully that the work would be done without charge. To our surprise, not one church responded. We had to fall back on suggestions from members of our own association.

One name mentioned was that of Minnie Fredinburg, a seventy-nine-year-old widow whose husband Roy had died years earlier. For more than two decades Minnie's modest little home had lacked the upkeep essential in a house buffeted by Oregon's fierce coastal storms. Minnie's only income came from Social Security. She accepted her situation with good humor, smiling about the morning-glory vine that poked its way through her living room floor. But she was very concerned about how long her house would remain livable. When anyone suggested that she move, her quiet reply was always: "I want to stay in my own home as long as I can."

Minnie was a member of the Assembly of God church, so I asked her pastor, Kenneth Frank, to go with me and find out what the association could do to help.

Minnie seemed amazed that any such good fortune might be hers. She took us first into the little bathroom. "The floor right here is kind of soft," she said, gingerly resting part of her weight on it. It was soft, all right; her foot went right through.

To a builder's eye, this was only one of endless problems. The old roof was hopeless; it would have to be replaced altogether. The house needed repainting inside and out. The bedroom floor had pulled away from the wall. When we pulled up some of the rotting floorboards, I could see that part of the foundation was giving way.

It was a far bigger job than any of us had contemplated, but never mind: Minnie would have a house that she could stay in. Winter storms delayed us somewhat, but when a core group of about ten builders got started, their enthusiasm fired others not directly connected with the building trade.

We got support and publicity from the local media. A septic service brought over portable toilets so that the crews could stay on-site while the bathroom fixtures were being replaced. A local restaurant sent over giant-size burgers complete with french fries and soft drinks—their way of saying, "We're with you." Owners of a rental shop lent their equipment without charge. A bricklayer

A PORTION OF THYSELF

put in an attractive brick wall behind the trash burner. Women members of the association took on the interior decorating. One lady who had been painting the kitchen went downtown for new curtains. "I've got enough paint on my hands," she said happily, "to match color!"

Minnie's church friends rallied to empty her cupboards, take down pictures, and store her personal belongings during the two weeks she would be out of the house, staying with her daughter's mother-in-law. Watching those ladies work, we decided we would never attempt a gift-renovation without the support of the recipient's church.

Our Builders Association picked up a tab of about one thousand dollars for materials, as well as donating labor and some of the supplies. "Hold it," one of the fellows would call out, "I've got boards just the right size for this in my shed at home." No business approach at all—just heart approach.

After the house was jacked up, refinished inside, roofed, and painted, other volunteers laid a sidewalk and planted shrubs. Finally her friends moved Minnie back. That was a deeply touching moment for all of us. Minnie looked at the new carpeting and the new baseboard heat. "I asked God to let me stay here awhile longer," she said in a faltering voice, "but what have I ever done for Him to deserve something so wonderful?" Minnie's church friends can tell you what she has done all through the years. Her faithful support of the church, her quiet kindness to others—her whole life has been a silent prayer.

So that was the first year. Our association decided on a project for the following Christmas. We were going to renovate a little hut that the Girl Scouts of Newport had been using for their meetings. Once again it would take time and energy, and caring and money, but all of us knew it would be more than worth it in terms of satisfaction, in closeness to one another, in shared happiness. I have come to believe that there is in each of us a kind of reservoir of kindness and unselfishness (the kingdom of God, perhaps?) just waiting to be tapped. When it is, one discovers that the rewards of giving are far greater, as the Bible says, than the satisfaction of being on the receiving end all the time.

Because so few people counted what they gave, the total cost of Minnie's Christmas present is uncertain. The actual figure might be somewhere between $7500 and $10,000. We did keep track of man (and woman) hours: 379, of which I can happily claim at least 40 as my own.

Could an effort like ours be duplicated elsewhere? Of course it could! There are thousands of Home Builders Associations throughout the land, and they are the ones who have ready access to the skills and materials that are required.

As for that notion that the best gift of all is something that comes out of the skill God has given us, a famous American, Ralph Waldo Emerson, once wrote: "The only gift is a portion of thyself.... Therefore the poet brings his poem; the shepherd, his lamb; the farmer, corn; the miner, a gem; the sailor, coral and shells; the painter, his picture...."

Imagine what a joy it was, then, for us as the roofer brought his tar; the electrician, his wiring; the carpenter, his lumber: the plumber, his pipes; the painter, his paint; the landscaper, his shrubs: the decorator, her artistry....

Christmas and businessmen? They can go together.

What Can I Give Him?

What can I give Him
Poor as I am?
If I were a shepherd,
I would give Him a lamb,
If I were a Wise Man,
I would do my part,—
But what I can I give Him,
Give my heart.

CHRISTINA ROSSETTI

A Long Way Home

BY MARIA DIDRICHSONS

Every year on Christmas Eve our family comes together to decorate our tree. One by one we hang the familiar ornaments on its deep-green branches, and when the tree is full and resplendent, we stop and wait, in silence. We watch while my husband, Rudy, unwraps the last decoration: an old, much-used paraffin emergency candle. Carefully Rudy reaches up and secures the burnt-down stub to the top of the tree. A match is struck, the wick takes to the flame, and at last our family is ready to celebrate another Christmas.

Another Christmas... While that squat candle burns briefly, I think of how little it resembles the slender tapers that flickered on the Christmas trees of my childhood in Riga, Latvia. I think of our last Christmas there in 1943, a year of uncertainty. World War II was raging. We Latvians had been caught in the middle of a bloody tug-of-war, first by the Soviet army, then the German, and what lay ahead we could not know.

Even so, my tall, sandy-haired Rudy and our little daughter, Alina, gathered around the tree at my parents' house. Small red apples dangled merrily among the ornaments, and a hand-painted porcelain angel sat serenely on top. The hand-twisted candles of red, yellow, green, and white gave a glow to the room as my mother read the Christmas story. We held hands as we sang "Silent Night."

"Look, Alina," said Mother to our tiny three-year-old with blond curls and curious eyes, "these candles remind us that Jesus brings light into our lives just as He brought light into the world. His hand is on us always."

Alina's eyes grew wide. She toddled straight to the tree, took a glass ornament in her small hand—and pulled as hard as she could. We had to run to keep the tree from falling, and the candles from burning the house down!

Another Christmas... In 1944 the tide of the war had turned and Russian artillery once again approached Riga. Though most civilians were evacuated from the city so they'd be safe from the shellings, we were not allowed to leave, for Rudy was a much-needed electrical engineer. At last, however, on October 1, Rudy, Alina, and I crowded onto a train, the final one to leave. Twelve days later the city fell to the Soviets.

Where did the train take us? To safety? No. To Berlin. To more bombs, more shellings. We stayed in a small rooftop apartment whose owner had fled. Each night we slept with our coats and shoes on, ready to run to the shelter as soon as the sound of sirens split the darkness. Berlin was bombed daily, and often three times a night.

That Christmas Eve I found Rudy putting on his heavy coat. Always a strong, quiet man, he now had a look of determination. "Where—?" I started, but he interrupted me.

"It's Christmas Eve," he said. "I'm going to get our tree."

He emptied the few belongings from our suitcase and went out the door. Rudy rode one of the few "underground" trains to the forest on the outskirts of the city, and there he found a tree just big enough to fit into the suitcase. Hours later he returned.

We placed the tree on a tabletop and we had our Christmas. Rudy read the Christmas story aloud from our Bible, and Alina was given her present, a hand-carved squirrel that Rudy had worked on for months. The back legs moved when Alina pulled on the string. In the dimness the three of us held hands and sang "Silent Night." And for a few hours it was—the sirens were stilled.

Another Christmas... We never did see our homeland again. Or those we loved. At the end of the war Latvia became a Soviet state. We had nowhere to go, and nowhere were we wanted. We became three of the thousands of European DPs—displaced persons—and as such were sent to a camp deep in the forests of West Germany. The years went by, one long, empty year after the other.

Five Christmas Eves later, 1949, we were still there. Even on that special day, camp routine never varied. As always, I arose at 4:00 a.m. to peel potatoes with the other camp women. This Christmas Rudy and I were expecting another child, and it was getting harder and harder to make my way to the kitchen through the dark of the morning. Our one meal a day was the never-changing menu of soup.

The forest winds were biting as we trudged from supper in the mess hall to the barracks where we shared one room with four other families. Alina was eight years old now. Her long blond braids fell in bright contrast to the gray of her ever-shrinking jacket.

I tried to get into a happy mood for Christmas, but my spirit felt as murky as the frozen slush we walked through in our camp-issued wooden shoes. Mother always said God's hand is on us, but where is He? I wondered. We want another child, but why now, here? Why have four years of prayers for a home gone unanswered? I prepared to face another dark Christmas.

Yet in our corner of the drafty tin-roofed barracks stood a proud little tree. It was against regulations to have one, but Rudy had sneaked to the forest once more to find it. Other camp men had done the same for their families. There were no decorations on this tree, no candles proclaiming light to the world. But we had our Bible.

As we read again how Jesus had been born in a stable, no less rude than where we were living now, and how soon after His birth the Holy Family was forced to take flight, I realized that we had our own good reasons to be thankful. We had almost no possessions, but compared to others in the camp, we were rich. We had three chipped enamel plates from which to eat our soup; others had to use tin cans. Alina had only one dress, one pair of underwear, and one pair of socks, but every night I had time to clean and mend them. Most of all, however, we had one another—and we still had faith and hope. They were enough to make Christmas bright.

Another Christmas... Three months after our son, Johnny, was born, we were notified that we had been selected for immigration to America. A congregation in Kansas City, Missouri, was sponsoring one family. They specified a family with small children—and Johnny was the youngest child in the camp. Not only that, but because children under six months of age were considered too frail for the long ocean journey, we were allowed to go quickly to America, on a plane! In October 1950, six years to the day after we'd arrived in Berlin under fire, we left Germany in an unpressurized cargo plane.

The people of Children's Memorial Lutheran Church in Kansas City embraced us. In the midst of a housing shortage, they found us a small room and paid the first month's rent. One member was a foreman at a factory, and he arranged a job for Rudy. On Thanksgiving, however, the foreman and his wife brought us a roast chicken, a pumpkin pie—and bad news: business was slow and all new workers were laid off.

The next day Rudy came back from the employment office and joined me at our table. "They had an opening for someone to make coffee boxes," he said with a small smile on his lips. "I got the job. It pays sixty-nine cents an hour."

"Coffee boxes?" I asked, puzzled. But I, too, smiled at our good fortune. Soon we learned that Rudy wasn't making coffee boxes; he was making coffins!

Christmas Eve in Kansas City was sunny, the air crisp but not cold. Johnny gurgled in my lap as I sat at the table, carefully counting our savings: one dollar, plus a few nickels and pennies. There was no question what we'd spend it for. This time I wanted to be the one who would bring home the Christmas tree.

The outside door clicked open as Alina bounced in. Her cheeks were flecked with crimson, as much from excitement as from the December chill

I carefully gathered the coins in my handkerchief and took her offered hand. We left the baby with a friendly neighbor and walked together to the street corner where a sign read CHRISTMAS TREES, $1 A FOOT."

The manager of this operation was a middle-aged man in a red cap and short wool jacket. "What can I get you?" he asked, turning from his last customer.

"We'd like the smallest tree you have," I replied.

He dug in the pile and pulled out an evenly grown deep-green spruce about two feet high. I saw sparks catch fire in Alina's eyes.

"How much?" I asked, my fingers playing nervously over those hard-saved coins.

"Two dollars," said the manager.

"You have nothing smaller?"

"No, lady." The man was gruff.

I could see the look of disappointment in Alina's eyes. We turned and started to walk away. But where were we to find another tree?

"Wait a minute," the manager called after us, his voice momentarily losing its edge. He shook out the little spruce and placed it carefully over Alina's shoulder. "Merry Christmas, little girl."

"Thank you, thank you very much," I whispered, and squeezed all the money I had into his hand. We turned again and walked home joyfully, a Christmas melody on our lips.

That night Rudy drilled a small hole in one of the orange crates we used for chairs and slid the stem of the miniature tree into it. There were no presents under that tree, but there were presents all around it: a warm room, a family, a home in a nation called America.

In the bottom of my suitcase I found an emergency candle, and Rudy tied it securely to the top of the tree. Alina stood between us, and Johnny sat on my lap as his father read the second chapter of Luke: " 'And it came to pass in those days, that there went out a decree.... Glory to God in the highest, and on earth, peace, good will toward men.' "

To our gathered family, those were not only words, they were our life. Peace—at last to be without fear, to feel safe, to be free. Good will to men—goodness of heart, help, kindness, love. All this we had experienced from the church people, the factory foreman, the Christmas tree man, the neighbors in this new land.

Then, somehow, the light of that small candle illumined all those dark Christmases past. At last I could see God's hidden hand protecting us from bombs in Berlin and working all things together to bring us from exile in the camp. And I have seen it in the years since, as our children have grown up and had children of their own.

Now when they come to our lovely home at Christmas, we have a tall, handsome tree, and we decorate it with shiny trimmings. But each year, every year, the highlight of Christmas Eve is the moment Rudy unwraps the burnt-down emergency candle. When it is burning again, I turn to my son just as I did on the evening of our first Christmas in America. "Look, Johnny," I say. "This candle reminds us that Jesus brings light into our lives just as He brought light into the world. His hand is on us always."

Precious Light

We light a thousand candles bright
around the earth today,
And all the beams will shine across
the heaven's grand display.
Dear brightest star o'er Bethlehem,
O let your precious light
Shine in with hope and peace toward men
in every home tonight.

SWEDISH CAROL

The Quiet People

BY THE EDITORS OF GUIDEPOSTS

I n this holy season, in every season, the Quiet People are everywhere, filling the nooks and crannies of human need. At Guideposts, readers from all over the country tell us about these people who go quietly about doing good work.

In Louisiana, at Springfield's Blood River Landing marina, there's a reclusive, jack-of-all-trades kind of fellow who lives in an old fishing boat that he himself salvaged and repaired.

It might be thought that a sixty-seven-year-old man who chooses to live apart from the world doesn't like people. But whatever Henry Bobak's feelings are about people in general, there can be no doubt about his feelings for children. He loves them.

One year Henry came across some scrap lumber. Nobody thought it was good for much of anything, but he had an urge to do something with it. "The Lord," Henry says, "gave me a pair of hands and He said, 'Use them.' " So Henry salvaged the lumber and, just as he'd done with the boat, began to saw and hammer and carve the scraps into shape. Pretty soon he'd made 150 wooden toys, all carefully pegged, sanded, and decorated with bright lead-free paint. Then he began to give them away—trains, trucks, tops, doll furniture, and other playthings—to kids in his area in great need of a toy or two in their lives.

At first Henry's actions roused a certain amount of suspicion. "Some people thought I was a nut. Maybe some still do," he says. "But I didn't let that hold me back. I knew what I wanted to get done, so I went to work and did it."

The suspicion didn't last, though, and before long, donations of woodworking tools and materials began showing up at Blood River Landing, along with help in making deliveries. Since then, Henry has distributed more than four thousand of his handmade toys.

Like it or not, he has developed quite a reputation. Even to the point that nowadays the Springfield post office delivers all mail addressed to Santa Claus to—you guessed it—Henry Bobak.

It's hard to imagine two men more different than Henry Bobak and Mike Greenberg. Mike lives in a Greenwich Village apartment in New York City and works as a media analyst for Grey Advertising in a midtown skyscraper. He's a man who has not forgotten the lean years of the Depression when he was growing up in Brooklyn—or the icy chill of the winter when as a youngster he lost his gloves. "Money was scarce. I was ashamed to ask for a new pair."

The memory of his cold hands is sharp for Mike, but even sharper is the memory of his father, who ran a bakeshop in a poor neighborhood. He remembers his dad slipping a few buns or cakes into the bags of customers who could afford only bread.

When they thanked him for it the next day, he would say, "A little mistake. Forget it, please."

When Mike's father died, he wanted to pay tribute to him in some special way—maybe by doing something that would reflect the generosity he had loved in his dad. That's when he started buying three pairs of warm gloves every payday, twice a month, winter and summer.

Each year since then, between Thanksgiving and the Hanukkah-Christmas holidays, Mike slips a canvas bag over his shoulder and makes five or six trips to the city's Bowery district. There he gives away dozens of pairs of gloves to the homeless men and women who live on the streets.

No one in the Bowery knows who Mike is, but after many winters of his holiday pilgrimages, the people there have given him a name: Gloves.

Sarah Kreinberg of Portland, Oregon, is fifty years younger than Mike—proof that you don't have to be grown-up to be a Quiet Person. One Christmas the seven-year-old heard about children going hungry in Ethiopia and decided to send them her own food.

When she learned that this wasn't practical, Sarah emptied her piggy bank and donated every nickel, dime, and quarter to Ethiopian relief through a fund set up by her church. But that wasn't enough for Sarah. A few days later she saw a news photo of an Ethiopian baby and learned that a local bank was matching funds contributed by local people for an airlift to the starving

Africans. Determined to earn more money to give, she hit upon the idea of making tree ornaments to sell.

Sarah's decorations were shiny red silk-covered "apples" glued to ice cream cones, which she carried from door to door in a basket. The little blond girl, with apple cheeks to match the apple ornaments, was a winning salesperson and a persistent one: she continued her fund-raising campaign after the holidays by selling candy.

To date, Sarah's gifts to Ethiopian children, combined with matching donations, amount to nearly $6,500. That's an unusual sum for a child to raise single-handedly. But then Sarah is an unusual youngster, one who has a special feeling for children who are having trouble staying alive. Since the age of fifteen months, she has lived with an inoperable brain tumor.

The people who report to us about the Quiet People they observe may be telling us about their own relatives—in Sarah's case it was her mother—or it could be about utter strangers. In the "stranger" category is John Williams, who described an afternoon on the bus he drives in Milwaukee.

A week or so before Christmas, John was making his usual run westbound on Wisconsin Avenue. At the Marquette High School stop he picked up a bunch of boys who headed noisily for the back of the bus, horsing around, wisecracking. *Kids*, thought John Williams, shaking his head.

A few stops later, John pulled up in front of the Milwaukee County Medical Complex grounds, where a woman was waiting. She looked to be about thirty-five years old and her dingy gray coat was tattered from collar to hem. When she came up the steps of the bus, John saw she was wearing only socks on her feet.

"Where are your shoes?" John blurted.

"Is this bus going downtown?"

"Eventually we'll get downtown," John answered, still staring at her feet, "but right now we're going west."

"I don't mind the extra ride, as long as I can get warm." The woman paid her fare and sat down in a front seat.

John couldn't help himself. "Where are your shoes?" he asked again. "You can't be out on a day like today without shoes."

The woman sat up straighter in the seat and smoothed her coat. "Now, mister, don't you worry. The good Lord'll take care of me. Always has. I had enough to buy shoes for my kids and that's what counts."

John couldn't believe it. Here was a woman who didn't have any shoes on, telling him to stop worrying.

Before long, the bus pulled up at the 124th and Bluemound stop, where the high school crowd got off to transfer to another bus that would take them to their suburban homes. All the kids got off by the rear door—except one. This boy walked slowly up the aisle, then stopped in front of the woman and handed her his leather basketball shoes. "Here, lady, you take these." With that, he stepped off the bus and into the 10-degree chill in his stocking feet.

And that was how John Williams came to see the quietest of the Christmas Quiet People in all of Milwaukee.

Love in Action

Christmas is love in action.... When you love someone, you give to them, as God gives to us. The greatest gift He ever gave was the person of His Son, sent to us in human form so that we might know what God the Father is really like! Every time we love, every time we give, it's Christmas.

DALE EVANS ROGERS

Christmas in Kuling

BY KATHERINE PATERSON

Every December I would put aside whatever book I was working on and write a short story for my husband, John, a Presbyterian pastor, to read aloud to the congregation on Christmas Eve. Although I often complained about writing to such an inexorable deadline, it was my opportunity each year to leave behind the busyness and commercial glitz of the season and find my way into the heart of the gospel story. The Christmas after my father died, writing the story took me back to a song I learned one frightening December many years ago.

My parents were missionaries in China then, my father the principal of a boys' school in the ancient walled city of Huai'an. We lived on the school grounds in a little Chinese house. Everyone else who lived inside our gate was Chinese. Lao Tzao, the gateman and his family; Mr. Li, my father's best friend and closest colleague, and his family; and Mrs. Liu, a widow, who taught women the Bible and how to read. Mr. Li's teenage daughter played with us, and almost by the time I could walk, I was toddling over to Mrs. Liu's house for lunch, where the meal was guaranteed to be Chinese.

My father and Mr. Li made frequent trips out into the countryside, riding donkeys along rutted dirt paths from village to village. Daddy's official title was evangelist but a lot of what he and Mr. Li, also a pastor, actually did was relief work, taking food and medicine to help the country people through drought, flood, and disease. Mr. Li was a classical scholar, and through him my father learned a great and enduring appreciation for Chinese history and culture.

Nearly every summer our family headed to Kuling, in the Lushan Mountains, about a week's journey from Huai'an. Its name no longer appears on maps of China because Kuling was a word made up by its founder, a play on the English word *cooling*. Established by a British missionary in the late nineteenth century as a haven from the punishing heat and humidity of east China's central plains, Kuling had over the years become a favorite spot for Chinese government officials.

In late June of 1937, when I was not quite five years old, we set off for Kuling. We went mostly by boat, but when we reached the foot of the mountain we got into sedan chairs and were carried on the shoulders of strong men up the dizzying stone steps carved into the steep mountainside. We settled into the rented vacation cottage, my brother and sister and I as happy to meet our summer friends as our parents were to meet theirs.

For the first week, all was peaceful. Then in early July an incident between Chinese and Japanese soldiers near the ancient capital of Peking (now Beijing) escalated. The Japanese took over

Peking and Tientsin (Tienjin). The war that was to become World War II had begun.

Despite the battles raging in the North, August was a quiet month in Kuling, except for the excitement in our house on the twenty-first when a second baby sister was born. That arrival was harder on me than the prospect of war. By the middle of September, when we had planned to start back for home, there was so much fighting that Daddy returned to Huai'an without us.

The Japanese must have known that Kuling was a favorite place of high-ranking Chinese officials, and the bombs began to fall while Daddy was gone. We dreaded nighttime when we knew the planes would come. The red-tiled roofs of Kuling had to be painted black. We pulled blackout curtains over our windows and listened in the darkness as the planes flew over, so low and loud that I thought the wheels were raking across our roof. Then we listened, hardly breathing, for the crash and explosion.

Shanghai fell in November, and in December, Nanking. What would happen next no one knew. The weather grew colder. Daddy had said he'd bring our winter clothes, but there was no sign of him. I missed my father terribly. There was no way of knowing when or if he would return. Travel was difficult if not impossible. The Japanese had closed all ports and taken control of the railways; riverboats were jammed and bandits roamed the countryside. There was no telephone service and mail seldom got through, so we didn't know if he was safe. Even though Mother tried to stay strong for us, we could sense her anxiety. When was he coming? How could we have Christmas without Daddy?

Then, miraculously, our father got back through the fighting to Kuling, bringing our winter clothes. Our parents did the best they could to make it seem like Christmas. We cut a holly bush and decorated it with homemade ornaments. I wish I could say that was Christmas enough, but I had set my heart on a beautiful American doll. Instead, both Elizabeth and I got Chinese-made harmonicas. I could only make a noise in mine by inhaling and exhaling. I had no hope of ever producing a tune.

But we did have music that Christmas. Some wise person gathered us frightened, unhappy children together into a choir to sing for the Christmas service. We learned a new carol, "There's a Song in the Air." We sang, "There's a tumult of joy o'er the wonderful birth, for the virgin's sweet boy is the Lord of the earth," and somehow the sounds of planes and detonating bombs seemed less threatening, the night behind the blackout curtains less dark. For wasn't the baby Jesus too born into a frightening, unsettled world?

Many years later, missing my father once again, I found myself singing those hopeful words, and I knew what I would write about for my husband's congregation. I used the carol that had comforted me long ago in China as the core of a story in which the narrator remembers his worst Christmas, after news has come of his older brother's death as a prisoner of war. His father refuses to go to church, even though the narrator, then nine, has been chosen to sing a solo.

"He can sing it for me right here in the kitchen," the father says. When the boy begins "There's a Song in the Air," his father explodes. "There's no singing in the sky," he shouts. "There's hate and suffering and cruel, cruel death!" But at the end of the story the narrator concludes that the song persists, "a melody of the most stubborn sweetness, for which we are never prepared...and someday it will find you...."

It still finds us, even today, in a world where, once again, none of us knows what the future will bring. "Ay! The star rains its fire while the beautiful sing, for the manger of Bethlehem cradles a king." Nothing, I believe, can silence that song or put out the light from that star.

There's a Song in the Air

In the light of that star lie the ages impearled;
And that song from afar has swept over the world.
Every hearth is aflame, and the beautiful sing
In the homes of the nations that Jesus is King!

JOSIAH HOLLAND

In Full Supply

BY JACQUELINE HEWITT ALLEN

Years and years ago, my grandmother told me a story out of her past that I always think of at gift-giving time, especially at Christmas. I remember sitting in her lap as dark-eyed little Sue Belle Johnson, my grandmother, explained how, shortly after the turn of the century, at remote and often lonely stations across the United States and overseas, missionaries and their families lived lives of hardship, privation, and isolation in their efforts to carry the gospel to people most of us would never know or see.

Probably at no time of the year were their feelings of isolation and loneliness more keenly felt than at Christmas. To remember them at this season, the custom in those days was for churches to send what were called "missionary barrels" to missionaries in remote locations.

The missionary and his wife would sit down with their children and make a list of things they wanted for Christmas. The list would include articles of clothing, toys, perhaps books or household utensils—whatever they especially needed but could not afford or could not find to buy. The list also included the ages of the children and their clothing sizes.

When completed, the list was sent to the missionary organization that helped sponsor them. The organization in turn sent it to a church, whose members would then take it upon themselves to acquire the items on the list.

My grandmother's church in Hattiesburg, Mississippi, was one of the churches that received such a Christmas list. That particular year, the list came from a missionary family in what was then called Indian Territory. The women of Grandmother's church, many of them, saw it as a holy task to choose an item and either buy it, make it, or donate money for its purchase.

On an appointed day all the requested items would be brought to the church, and the women would check the items against the list, wrap them, and pack them into a big wooden-staved, double-ended barrel. The barrel would then be shipped in time for the family to receive it by Christmas.

Not everybody in Grandmother's church cooperated. While the women were packing the missionary barrel, one of the more well-to-do women of the church walked into the room carrying a coat. "I've got this coat of my husband's that I want to give to you," she announced offhandedly. "I'm going to buy him a new one."

Grandmother was appalled. She didn't say anything, but she was thinking plenty: these other people have worked hard to get these articles, some have sacrificed to get them, and here this woman is in effect bragging, "I'm so rich I can go out and buy another coat."

The more she thought about the woman's haughtiness, the more irritated Grandmother became. *She's just ridding herself of an unwanted castoff,* Grandmother said to herself. *What kind of Christmas attitude is that?* Grandmother was furious—about the coat and with the woman.

A coat was not on the missionary family's list, and the women packing the barrel had no intention of putting the coat in it. But after all the requested items had been carefully placed in the barrel, there was still room left.

"Well," one of the women said, "let's put that coat in. It might help keep the other articles tight, keep them from bouncing around and maybe breaking."

So they folded the coat, packed it in, and closed the barrel. Then they shipped it to the family out in the Indian Territory.

Weeks passed. Christmas came and went. Then a letter arrived at the church: the family's thank-you, written by the missionary's wife. "Dear Friends," it began, "we want to thank you for the barrel."

She then recounted how her husband and their three children had driven to the railhead to pick up the barrel, had brought it home and placed it upright in the middle of the living room floor in their little cabin, waiting for Christmas. The children were so excited they danced around it in gleeful anticipation.

Then on the day before Christmas a fierce winter storm blew in. It quickly developed into a blizzard, with snow so thick and winds so furious that the entire outdoors seemed a blowing, blinding mass of white. Shortly before suppertime, as the blizzard raged, there was a banging on the front door, and when the missionary opened the door to see what the banging was, there stood an old man, grizzled, ill clad for the freezing temperature, shivering and covered with snow.

"I'm lost," the man said. "Could I come in for a while?"

The missionary opened the door wider and said, "Of course. Come on in."

After supper, it was all but impossible to contain the children, they were so excited and eager to open the barrel. But their mother managed to get them bedded down, explaining that they would have to wait a little longer, since it would be terribly impolite to open the barrel, pull out the presents, and distribute them with the old man there. "There's nothing for him," the mother said. "It's just the things we put on our list. We'll have to wait till the man leaves."

The next morning, Christmas morning, the family arose and found that the storm had not abated; the winds were as wild as the night before. The mother fixed a special breakfast for everyone, and when breakfast was over, they watched and waited for the storm to end so that the old man could be on his way and they could break open the barrel.

Afternoon came and the storm was still raging, but the children just couldn't wait any longer. So the missionary and his wife explained to the old man that the barrel had been packed many weeks earlier and contained Christmas presents for the family only. They apologized profusely, and when the old man nodded and said he understood, the missionary turned to the barrel and began to break open the uppermost end of it.

The family then began pulling out, one by one, the items they had asked for on their Christmas list. Each item was clearly marked so that they all knew whose present it was. Everyone was excited. The clothes, the toys, everything, were exactly what the family had requested. Everyone was happy and pleased, while the old man sat and watched.

Finally they reached the bottom of the barrel. There on the bottom, at the end of the barrel that had been uppermost when the women packed it, was an item the family didn't recognize. It was nothing they had asked for. When the missionary reached deep into the barrel to pull out the object, he could see it was a man's coat. He held it up. It looked to be about the size of the old man. "Try it on." The man took it and slipped it on. It fit perfectly. "It must be for you," the missionary told him, smiling.

"How did you ever know," the missionary wife's letter concluded, "that we would need a man's coat for Christmas? Thank you all so very much."

By the time she finished reading the letter, my grand-mother said, she was nearly overcome with awe. The cast-off coat that had needed a new owner had found one. An old man who had needed a warm coat had been given one. A family who had taken in a lost stranger and needed a special present for him had been provided with one. It was all too marvelous to comprehend, my grandmother said. Surely God, in His wondrous omniscience, she said, had wrought a miracle with a gift she had thought unworthy.

When she finished her story, Grandmother took my hands in hers and said, "I learned that day that I had been wrong—and that I should never despise a gift that God can use."

As Christmas approaches again, I'm remembering once more my grandmother's words. As I choose presents to give this Christmas, I am hoping that they will be gifts that will make the recipients happy and me proud to give. But most of all I am praying that, whatever they are, whomever they're for, they will be exactly the gifts that God can use.

The Joy of Giving

The joy of brightening other lives,
bearing each other's burdens,
easing others' loads and
supplanting empty hearts and lives
with generous gifts
becomes for us the magic of Christmas.

W. C. JONES

The Old Steamer Trunk

BY SARAH HUDSON-PIERCE

Christmas had never meant much to me growing up in South West City, Missouri. We had almost no extended family. My grandparents had died years earlier and my father was an only child. Though I had one sister, I felt rootless.

I also had no self-esteem. During class assignments I felt inferior to classmates who had so much to proclaim about their family histories. One boy proudly spoke of his father having fought in World War II; others told of ancestors arriving in covered wagons.

My taciturn parents had never had much to say about our heritage. All I knew was both of them worked very hard to provide for our meager existence. Father plowed all day behind mules just to feed us. So when my teacher called on me I slumped in my seat and let someone else tell of his or her relatives' accomplishments.

When class resumed after Christmas week and others excitedly spoke of their many gifts, I remained silent. For me Christmas meant only one gift. One year it was homemade candy, another it was a toy watch.

But when I was nine I was blessed with the gift that would sustain me for life. It was 1957 and that Christmas Eve we sat around our blazing cast-iron woodstove. I received my gift—a wool scarf—and Father read the Bible to us by the light of a kerosene lamp.

As the flickering lamp cast shadows about the room I found myself staring at the steamer truck that sat in a corner, an embroidered scarf covering its rounded lid. It was kept locked, safe from childish hands. I had long begged to look inside, but Father would shake his head.

"Nothing to play with, child," he said. "Just a lot of old stuff." That only whetted my curiosity, and I prayed God would somehow get my father to open it. On that Christmas I felt even more compelled to see what was inside. I clung to Mother's waist almost in tears, pleading for her to have Father open it.

Finally he got up and said, "Seeing it's Christmas and all, I guess it won't do any harm."

He took a key from a high shelf, knelt, and unlocked the trunk. As the lid creaked open, the first thing I saw was an old tobacco can. Father showed me the blond curls inside it, saved from his first haircut. When he saw my delight it seemed to open some kind of emotional dam within him. He began telling about the other items he took out of the trunk. He proudly showed an old sepia-tinted picture of his father, George Washington McClellan Hudson, my circuit-riding preacher grandpa, born in 1865 in Indiana. In yellowed journals, in fine cursive script, my grandpa wrote how in 1888 he came to Licking, Missouri, where he met Sarah Alice Ritz-Hudson, my namesake. Their wedding picture on stiff board showed a handsome couple.

I was thrilled and captivated all through Christmas Day as I studied the trunk's treasures. I found a tintype of Great-grandfather Ritz, who had emigrated to America from Bern, Switzerland, in 1851. His diary spoke of his despair of ever seeing land again as he spent three months crossing the Atlantic on a small sailing ship. I learned of my great-grandpa Hudson, who had brought the steamer trunk over from Hull, England, in 1830. And I was fascinated by my great-grandfather Morris, a doctor during the Civil War.

I fondly fingered Great-grandmother Hudson's hand-carved wooden crochet hooks, and reverently touched hair and scraps of my great-grandmother Ritz's burial clothing that were mailed to my grandmother Hudson, who had been unable to attend the funeral.

I held the golden locket that contained the picture my mother cherished most—of her mother, who died of typhoid fever when Mother was only two. And I was told how my grandparents had raced their wagon in the Oklahoma land rush and how my mother was born in an underground Indian dwelling in 1906, about the time Oklahoma became a state.

The wonderful gifts in the old steamer trunk planted a seed of self-esteem that would blossom and grow, enriching my life. Not only did I feel pride in my ancestry, but I had ample stories to tell my schoolmates. Now I truly felt the richest girl in class.

Christmas Treasures

There is nothing quite so deeply satisfying as the solidarity of a family united across the generations and miles by a common faith and history.

SARA WENGER SHENK

When Time Stood Still

BY ADELA ROGERS ST. JOHNS

When it comes to God's guidance, which it does every day, every hour, there are many ways we can seek it.

More and more often, more and more surely, with more and more conviction as my need and my faith grow, I have learned to depend on it.

Stand ye still.

Always those words come to me when I ask for guidance, wherever I happen to be, no matter how rushing and noisy it may be inside my mind and out. For to those words I owe the life of my oldest son, Mac.

One December night I awoke suddenly and completely, sitting straight up in bed. I was sure somebody had called me. When I switched on the light, my clock said 3:15. Getting up, I prowled—a niece, a nephew, one younger son were sleeping in the house. Everyone seemed safe and peaceful.

I do not hear voices, nor see lights, nor catch the echo of bells. But when guidance comes, something irresistible seems to take over. Now the call was distinct in my mind—a call for help.

In the living room I saw the Christmas tree. Next to the fireplace it stood, slim and green. Tomorrow we'd hang it with bright colors and put the Christmas angel on the top—the one that had been my grandmother's. It was the season of peace on earth, goodwill to men, but there was no peace on earth, this December of 1944. It was the month of the Battle of the Bulge, Bastogne, the Ardennes. My brothers were marines in the Pacific, my oldest son in France with Patton.

I went back to bed. The call was not from within my home's safe walls. The clock now said 3:25. But it was a different time on islands in the Pacific, on the battlefields of Europe. So I did what, whenever it is possible, is my first step in asking for guidance. I got my Bible from under the detective story with which I'd read myself to sleep, shut my eyes, and said, "Father, let me find Your word meant for me. I think one of Your other children needs Your help. I am far away from whoever it is, but You are near us both. Speak to us now through Your Word."

In guidance, my experimentation leads me to believe that inner quietness is the first requirement. And the most difficult. Nobody wants to be quiet. Not many of us want to be silent and listen. Prayer is an audience, not an audition; nevertheless, we start telling our Father about the problem and how He ought to solve it.

That's why, when I ask for guidance, to keep my own mind still, I read something: a prayer, a book of inspiration, mostly the Bible. Then I try to be quiet for as long as I am able, in my mind

I mean, which is about one minute and forty-two seconds; two minutes at the most, as it is with most people. Then I ask, with all the expectation and humility that I can generate.

That night I opened the Bible. Just anywhere, where it fell apart.

"Stand ye still, and see the salvation of the Lord with you...fear not, nor be dismayed, for the Lord will be with you" (2 Chronicles 20:17 KJV).

Stand ye still. It stood out from the page like copy on a billboard.

And so, simply and directly, I began to pray.

I knew now from whom the call had come, as it had come for many years in many dark nights.

"Father," I prayed, "Your guidance now goes to my son, somewhere in battle, somewhere in danger. Your word goes forth to him and will accomplish what You please for him, which is his safety and his guidance, the light to his feet."

Stand ye still.

I knew, I really did, that this was my guidance and would be my son's. That it had come to me through a channel kept open by prayer and longing and seeking. I went back to sleep in peace.

At breakfast, I told everyone what had taken place. Then it came to me that as it was so near Christmas and everybody always remembers things around Christmas, perhaps Mac would remember something about that early morning hour. So to his APO number I wrote, describing the experience.

His reply reached me soon after Christmas. It said:

Yes, I can remember. I was the leader on an I&R (Intelligence and Reconnaissance) platoon; we were out ahead of our regiment, somewhere in the German area, to see if it were safe to move forward. We were moving cautiously, but General Patton was always in a hurry so we were trotting along as fast as we dared.

All of a sudden it was as though something told me to stop. To stand still. And as I did, out of the corner of my eye, I saw a place on a tree where somebody had chopped off the bark and scrawled in paint the word *Minen*. So I knew it was a mine field. A German soldier had put that sign up to warn his own troops.

We went back faster than we'd come out, and called up the mine detector squad and, sure enough, there were mines enough to blow up the whole platoon, maybe the Third Army. If I hadn't stopped (and I had to be standing dead-still to see it because it faced the other way) I wouldn't be writing this letter. And we wouldn't have had any Christmas, merry or otherwise.

Maybe you will have another explanation for this!
But to this day it has made a working Christian out of my son Mac. To me it was God's guidance. The voice of His love for us coming through to us.

The first time you receive guidance you will know the difference. You can mistake rhinestones for diamonds, but you can never mistake a diamond for a rhinestone. I know what is true guidance when my mind, my consciousness, whatever we call our mental process, is thinking utterly and completely with some thought that I know I have not thought. This comes when the mind that was in Christ Jesus for which we have prayed takes over.

In the Stillness

God is our refuge and strength,
an ever-present help in trouble.
Therefore we will not fear....
Be still and know that I am God.

PSALM 46:1-2, 10 MSG

At Christmas Town

SAM MCGARRITY

H ave you ever spent Christmas in a place that linked you so closely to the season that you actually felt at peace with the Christmas spirit? Let me explain. I'm one of those single people who never quite fit anywhere during the holidays. For me, it's the season to feel awkward, and as jolly as I may appear outwardly, inwardly I'm relieved when Christmas is over.

One year I'd planned to sleep through Christmas Day, just as I did the Christmas before. My editor ruined that plan.

Christmas was almost upon me, when one afternoon he said, "Sam, we want you and The Pup to drive down to McAdenville, North Carolina, during Christmas week. It's a small town just outside of Charlotte. The mill, it seems, has a chaplain, and he's been in touch with us about some sort of light extravaganza there. He claims that McAdenville becomes Christmas Town in December. It's supposed to be famous. See what it's all about, would you?"

As I steered my 1978 Volkswagen van—which still had no heater—south toward McAdenville, I grumbled to The Pup, the Eskimo spitz who travels with me, "Most towns have lights at Christmas, don't they? Why would this one be any different? Famous, he said! It's so obscure it's not even in the road atlas."

I doubted I'd find much there. It would be damp and miserable. I grew up in the South, where it never snows at Christmas—just rains. And the wet cold seeps through and chills you to the bone. Gray skies threatening rain welcomed me to the Southland.

In Gaston County, North Carolina, I turned off Interstate 85 and left behind the rush of traffic speeding to keep pace with the holiday frenzy. I'd arrived.

Coasting down Main Street, which wound like a skein of yarn past neat yards and well-kept homes that proclaimed the past, I noticed that each had been tastefully decorated with traditional greenery, poinsettias, wreaths, and bows. Porch swings and rockers silently waited for warmer days and company to come "sit a spell." They reminded me of the Sundays when our family used to sit and rock on my great-uncle's porch in Georgia.

In the heart of town, where Main Street forked, two blocks of shops offered dining out, gifts, banking, and barbering. Three brick buildings, the original mills built in 1881 by Rufus Y. McAden and around which the town had developed, now housed the headquarters of Stowe-Pharr Mills, a family-owned textile business with plants in four states and the Netherlands. Stowe-Pharr had grown from a two-hundred-man operation, salvaged after the Depression from McAdenville's closed mills and dying town, to an international business employing about five thousand people. It was the owner and employer of McAdenville.

I walked The Pup along the nearby south fork of the Catawba River, then met with Billy Miller, the chaplain of Stowe-Pharr, who, I hoped, would tell me why this sleepy little town of 960 people, four churches, and one filling station was a Christmas landmark. Instead, standing tall like a steeple and seeming about as serene, he asked with a twinkle in his eye, "Want to come along on a Santa Mission tomorrow morning?"

I'd never heard of such a thing. "How early?" I asked.

"Eight o'clock."

That sounded pretty early to me. I thought Santa conducted his missions at night, but I said, "Okay, I'll go."

In the meantime, it was almost 5:00 p.m. when Billy Miller and I left his office to tour the town. "The lights will be coming on," he announced.

Click, click, click. Suddenly McAdenville glowed in the dusk as I watched a spectacle of 340,000 red, white, and green lights turn on. Circling through the town's magnolias, its pines and cedars and dogwoods, the fantasy of lights stretched up and down Main Street, from yard to yard, around the community center, the churches, around the mill buildings and the lake.

And as night approached, so did the people—in cars from Virginia, Georgia, South Carolina, Tennessee, and the "Ta'

Heel State." Bumper-to-bumper, like a graceful red ribbon, they followed the glistening trees and decorated doors through McAdenville. It would have sent tingles through the Grinch (the one who stole Christmas, remember?).

Walking along the streets of Christmas Town with The Pup prancing beside me, I listened and hummed along with the chrono-chimes that pealed carols into the air. They spoke to us, "Fall on your knees! Oh, hear the angel voices!"

A sense of joy slowly stole inside me. It didn't matter that I was alone. I wasn't really. There were all of these people waving to me from cars and the sidewalk, wishing me "Merry Christmas!" Children stopped me on the street and asked to pet The Pup. "He's so-o-o soft. Purty dawg," they crooned.

We drifted along, listening to the exclamations of "Well, I declare!" over the lights and the manger scene. We watched a pretend snowman being lovingly hugged by a real little boy. I sang "Jingle Bells" with a couple of kids from out of town just because it seemed appropriate on such a magical night. And I felt myself actually beginning to look forward to the Santa Mission.

The next morning, I joined the Santa Mission in the research lab of Stowe-Pharr. Lab workers had forgone an office party in order to supply some cheer to a young family whose baby had been in and out of the hospital. Nine of us, lugging shopping bags of gifts and boxes of clothes, followed at the heels of Billy Miller, who knew the troubles of everyone in town and led us to the home of this particular family in need. A doll hung from the opening of one large sack; a shovel poked from another. One lady carried a tricycle. My arms were aching! Billy Miller hadn't mentioned that this mission would require muscles.

At a back door, we heard a young woman scolding and hurrying a protesting little boy into the front room. We waited silently. Then she appeared and welcomed us in. "Oh," she faltered, "how can I ever thank you! You don't know how much this means..."

I knew. We were all silent, trying to blink the tears from our eyes, trying to swallow the lumps in our throats. We all remembered hard times and the generosity of friends easing us through holidays of hopelessness. I remembered the down coat friends gave me one Christmas when I couldn't afford a heavy coat. "We're tired of seeing you wear all those sweaters, Sam," they told me as I peeled off the Christmas wrap. That was when I lived with those friends because I couldn't afford a home either.

Silently we each hugged this young mother of three children. I wanted to tell her that life would get better, but I felt embarrassed. I hoped an embrace would express what I couldn't say. And then we bowed our heads for Billy Miller's Christmas blessing over that staggering kitchen table. Before we filed out, he handed her an envelope containing $209, another gift from the research department. So that was a Santa Mission.

As I visited in the mills and talked with spinning overhaulers and pin operators, oilers and crillers, inspectors and packers and supervisors and plant managers, I heard of other Santa Missions. The Stowe-Pharr carpenters had collected $1,700 for a colleague in need. Someone in Plant No. 46 had dressed up in a Santa suit and collected donations for a sick child. The McAdenville Women's Club had provided Christmas for another child. Two sisters had decorated a plant wall with a Christmas scene "just to help people get in the holiday mood."

At holiday gatherings throughout the mills, workers exchanged gifts over homemade casseroles and desserts. They swapped memories of Christmases past. And as one young man in a buffet line whispered to me, "People seem to care about each other here," I began to understand that Christmas Town was more than just lights and decorations.

I should mention, though, that the lights too were a symbol of caring that began with Mr. William J. Pharr, the company leader from 1939 to 1981. "He was a man who loved people," I was told over and over. "He would go up to workers and hug them and tell them how much they meant to him. It didn't matter how much oil or grease or lint they were wearing that day. That's the kind of man he was." Under the careful direction of his wife, Catherine Stowe Pharr, and with the help of a team of men, the lighting of McAdenville's trees became a thirty-three-year tradition that grew from nine trees to 348. And each year, Stowe-Pharr pays the electric bill.

In 1950 Mr. Pharr brought the Yule Log Celebration to McAdenville. And along with parents, children, and a brass band, I joined in the fun of following the thirty-ninth log dragged up Main Street.

It was a rainy, misty night—the kind that would ordinarily have chilled me to the bone. But I felt surrounded by warm people whose compassion for one another was ushering in the spirit of the Christ child. These were people who were used to being told they were loved by the company's chief executive officer. I know, because I read those words by him in the company newspaper. These were people who were comfortable praying together. I know, because I bowed my head with them that night in front of the burning Yule log as Catherine Ann Carstarphen, the chief executive officer's wife, led us in prayer. These were people who faced their joys and sorrows with a chaplain who advised them and knelt with them and joked with them.

This was a different world from the big city I had just left, a city where escaping Christmas would have been easy. Here there was no escaping it. Nor did I want to. I already felt a part of it, and I wanted to share it with people I loved.

And so, on Christmas Eve, I decided to continue on in the spirit of the season. "We're going down to Georgia," I told The Pup, "to visit Grandmother and my aunt and cousins." We didn't have gifts, but maybe just a caring spirit would be gift enough. I'd rediscovered it there in Christmas Town, and I was going to be sure to take it with me on the road.

Christmas Spirit

Best of all, Christmas means a spirit of love,
a time when the love of God and the love
of our fellow men should prevail...a time when
our thoughts and deeds and the spirit
of our lives manifest the presence of God.

GEORGE F. MCDOUGALL

A "Sensible" Christmas

BY HENRY APPERS

F or as long as I could remember our family had talked about a sensible Christmas. Every year, my mother would limp home from shopping or she would sit beside the kitchen table after hours of baking, close her eyes, catch her breath, and say, "This is the last time I'm going to exhaust myself with all this holiday fuss. Next year we're going to have a sensible Christmas."

And always my father, if he was within earshot, would agree. "It's not worth the time and expense."

While we were kids, my sister and I lived in dread that Mom and Dad would go through with their rash vows of a reduced Christmas. But if they ever did, we reasoned, there were several things about Christmas that we ourselves would like to amend. And two of these were, namely, my mother's Uncle Lloyd and his wife, Aunt Amelia.

Many a time Lizzie and I wondered why families had to have relatives, and especially why it was our fate to inherit Uncle Lloyd and Aunt Amelia. They were a sour and a formal pair who came to us every Christmas, bringing Lizzie and me handkerchiefs as gifts and expecting in return silence, respect, service, and for me to surrender my bedroom.

Lizzie and I had understood early that Great-uncle Lloyd was, indeed, a poor man, and we were sympathetic to this. But we dared to think that even poverty provided no permit for them to be stiff and unwarm and a nuisance in the bargain. Still we accepted Great-uncle Lloyd and Great-aunt Amelia as our lot, and they were, for years, as much the tradition of Christmas as mistletoe.

Then came my first year in college. It must have been some perverse reaction to my being away, but Mom started it. This was to be the year of the sensible Christmas. "By not exhausting ourselves with all the folderol," she wrote me, "we'll at last have the energy and the time to appreciate Christmas."

Dad, as usual, went along with Mom but added his own touch. We were not to spend more than a dollar for each of our gifts to one another. "For once," Dad said, "we'll worry about the thought behind the gift, and not about its price."

It was I who suggested that our sensible Christmas be limited to the immediate family, just the four of us. The motion was carried. Mom wrote a gracious letter to Great-uncle Lloyd explaining that what with my being away in school and for one reason and another we weren't going to do much about Christmas, so maybe they would enjoy it more if they didn't make their usual great effort to come. Dad enclosed a check, an unexpected boon.

I arrived home from college that Christmas wondering what to expect. A wreath on the front door provided a fitting nod to the season. There was a Christmas tree in the living room, and I must admit that, at first, it made my heart twinge. Artificial, the tree was small and seemed without character when compared to the luxurious, forest-smelling firs of former years. But the more I looked at it, with our brightly wrapped dollar gifts under it, the friendlier it became, and I began to think of the mess of real trees, and their fire threat, and how ridiculous, how really unnatural it was to bring a living tree inside a house anyway. Already the idea of a sensible Christmas was getting to me.

Christmas Eve Mom cooked a good but simple dinner, and afterward we all sat together in the living room. "This is nice," Lizzie purred, a-snuggle in the big cabbage rose chair.

"Yes," Dad agreed. "It's quiet. I'm not tired out. For once, I think I can stay awake until church."

"If this were last Christmas," I reminded Mom, "you'd still be in the kitchen with your hours of 'last-minute' jobs. More cookies. More fruitcake." I recalled the compulsive way I used to nibble at Mom's fruitcake. "But I never really liked it," I confessed with a laugh.

"I didn't know that," Mom said. She was thoughtful for a moment. Then her face brightened. "But Aunt Amelia—how she adored it!"

"Maybe she was just being nice," Lizzie said undiplomatically.

Then we fell silent. Gradually we took to reading. Dad did slip off into a short snooze before church.

Christmas morning we slept late, and once up we breakfasted before advancing to our gifts. And what a time we had with those! We laughed merrily at our own originality and cleverness. I gave Mom a cluster-pin that I had fashioned out of aluminum measuring spoons and had adorned with rhinestones. Mother wore the pin all day or, at least, until we went out to Dempsey's.

At Dempsey's, the best restaurant in town, we had a wonderful, unrushed feast. There was only one awkward moment just after the consommé was served. We started to lift our spoons. Then Dad suggested that we say grace and we all started to hold hands around the table as we always do at home, and then we hesitated and drew our hands back, and then, in unison, we refused to be intimidated by a public eating place and held hands and said grace.

Nothing much happened the rest of the day. In the evening I wandered into the kitchen, opened the refrigerator, poked around for a minute, closed the door, and came back to the living room.

"That's a joke," I reported, with no idea at all of the effect my next remark would have. "I went out to pick at the turkey."

In tones that had no color, Mother spoke. "I knew that's what you went out there for. I've been waiting for it to happen."

No longer could she stay the sobs that now burst forth from her. "Kate!" Dad cried, rushing to her.

"Forgive me. Forgive me," Mom kept muttering.

"For what, dear? Please tell us."

"For this terrible, dreadful, sensible Christmas."

Each of us knew what she meant. Our Christmas had been as artificial as that Christmas tree; at some point the spirit of the day had just quietly crept away from us. In our efforts at common sense we had lost the reason for Christmas and had forgotten about others; this denied Him whose birthday it was all about. Each of us, we knew full well, had contributed to this selfishness, but Mom was taking the blame.

As her sobs became sniffles and our assurances began to take effect, Mom addressed us more coherently, in Mom's own special incoherent way. "I should have been in the kitchen last night instead of wasting my time," she began, covering up her sentimentality with anger. "So you don't like my fruitcake, Harry? Too bad. Aunt Amelia really adores it! And Elizabeth, even if she doesn't, you shouldn't be disrespectful to the old soul. Do you know who else loves my fruitcake? Mrs. Donegan down the street loves it. And she didn't get her gift from me this year. Why? Because we're being sensible." Then Mom turned on Dad, wagging her finger at him. "We can't afford to save on Christmas, Lewis! It shuts off the heart."

That seemed to sum it up.

Yet, Lizzie had another way of saying it. She put it in a letter to me at school, a letter as lovely as Lizzie herself. "Mom feels," Lizzie wrote, "that the strains and stresses are the birth pangs of Christmas. So do I. I'm certain that it is out of our efforts and tiredness and turmoil that some sudden, quiet, shining, priceless thing occurs each year, and if all we produce is only a feeling as long as a flicker, it is worth the bother."

Just as my family came to call that The Christmas That Never Was, the next one became the Prodigal Christmas. It was the most festive, and the most frazzling, time in our family's history—not because we spent any more money, but because we threw all of ourselves into the joy of Christmas. In the woods at the edge of town we cut the largest tree we'd ever had. Lizzie and I swathed the house in greens. Delicious smells came from the kitchen as Mom baked and baked and baked.... We laughed and sang carols and joked. Even that dour pair, Great-uncle Lloyd and Great-aunt Amelia, were almost, but not quite, gay. Still, it was through them that I felt that quick surge of warmth, that glorious "feeling as long as a flicker," that made Christmas meaningful.

We had just sat down in our own dining room and had reached out our hands to one another for our circle of grace. When I took Great-aunt Amelia's hand in mine, it happened. I learned something about her and giving that, without this Christmas, I might never have known.

The hand that I held was cold. I became aware of how gnarled her fingers were, how years of agonizing arthritis had twisted them. Only then did I think of the handkerchiefs that Lizzie and I had received this year, as in all the years before. For the first time I saw clearly the delicate embroidery, the painstaking needlework—Great-aunt Amelia's yearly gift of love to, and for, us.

Gifts of Love

To receive a gift, molded from love and sacrifice,
selected with care and tied up with all
the excitement the giver has to offer,
is indeed rare. They don't come along often,
but when they do, cherish them.

ERMA BOMBECK

The Christmas Expedition

A s a young man of fifteen, I lived with my parents
and fourteen brothers and sisters on a farm that
was the closest to the North Pole in all of Alberta,
Canada. The nearest town of any size was eighty miles away.
We raised and preserved our own food, made our own clothes,
even sheared our own sheep to get the wool to make our mittens
and socks.

It was a hard life—those Depression years over half a
century ago—and yet a beautiful one. Often as I plowed furrows
for planting in the spring, I would watch the brown loam turning
beneath the blade and the birds soaring overhead in the brilliant
blue sky, and I'd feel like throwing back my head and singing—
and often I did.

My father made his living by farming and running a
general store. But when Sunday came, all work—and play—
stopped. My father was a lay preacher for a Baptist congregation, and the whole family spent four hours at church
every Sunday. We weren't allowed to play ball or even
shine our shoes on Sunday. I hated Sundays. I hated my
father's strictness.

My father would have liked nothing better than for me to be a preacher too. But I was having none of that. It seemed to me that all my father had ever received for his devotion to God was a lot of people's problems—and never an extra dime to call his own. Besides that, his God cooped you up and quieted you down. Well, that sort of somber, settled-down obedience was not for me. God clearly played no personal part in my high-spirited life.

Christmases were festive occasions in our house, with food and games and family fun. But there were never any what I considered real presents, only little paper bags with some hard candy and an orange, some raisins and some nuts. Maybe there'd be a dime, or even a quarter, inside if the crops had been good.

But as the Christmas of 1936 approached, I decided that things were going to be different. I devised a plan to make some money and buy some real, store-bought presents for everyone. I convinced my brother-in-law Metro, who was twenty-five, that we should travel north into the wilderness and bring back fish from Primrose Lake. This year, we'd heard, men were fishing through the ice with nets, scooping up even more fish than usual, fish that Metro and I could bring back to sell to shoppers stocking up on food for the holidays.

I was overjoyed at the thought of the money we'd make. Thirty, forty, maybe even fifty dollars—a huge sum for such hard times: no little brown bags for my family this year!

But my father intervened. "I'd rather you didn't go, son," he said. "Not in this weather, into territory where you've never been before. The horses are tired and you could be putting them, and yourself, in danger. We have enough food and money to get by."

But I was stubborn. Danger was the furthest thing from my mind. And my days of just "getting by" were over. I promised my father we'd be back soon (*and rich*, I thought to myself), and Metro and I prepared for the trip. Metro readied his own bobsled and team of horses. I harnessed our docile red gelding, Tom, and our gentle gray mare, Queen, into the doubletree shaft that held them to my bobsled. Neither Tom nor Queen was exactly what you'd call stamped with fire, but they were good horses who had served us steadily, and they could certainly do the job I had in mind.

We set off for the first of five days of travel, five days in which the light came late and darkness early. It was slow going— we had to break our way through snow often two feet deep, over icy expanses marked by gnarled scrub pines and jutting rocks. At night we made camp and slept in shifts, one of us always awake to tend our fire and keep the timber wolves at bay. The wolves were always at our heels, their eerie howling breaking through the moonlit silence.

At dusk on the fifth day, we reached our destination. Primrose Lake—its name sounded like soft blossoms and lapping blue waters, but now its surface glinted icy-white and diamond-hard for miles in front of us.

To our dismay there were a number of other people there too, obviously with the same idea. Metro and I hurried to join them, and for several days we slept with the fishermen in a shack near the lake. We covered the horses with burlap blankets and put them in an old log shelter.

We worked all through the week, hacking out openings in the six-inch thickness of ice, dangling bait into the water, then scooping the fish into nets. It was tedious, tiring work; we were relieved when our sleds were full of northern pike, whitefish, perch, and jackfish.

At last it was time to leave the ice and start for home. Just as we were making last-minute preparations, I heard a dull, thudding sound reverberating in the distance. Thunder? I hurried to insert the connecting pin that anchored the horses' stays to the sled.

I patted the flanks of Tom and Queen. How tired they seemed. But I knew they'd get us home all right—as long as they weren't called on to do much more than that.

I climbed aboard the sled. All I wanted to do now was to get home. Something, I didn't know what, was making me uneasy.

"Let's travel on the ice for a while," Metro said. "It will be easier." He waved a mittened hand and set off. I moved my team out behind him, the sled creaking under its heavy load.

We clopped along about a quarter of a mile out from shore, and soon saw two men heading out to where we'd been. "How's the fishing?" they called.

"Not worth much now," Metro called back. "Lots of fellas were here last week."

At that instant, as the sled shuddered beneath me, I heard the same deep thudding sound again, but this time I knew it wasn't thunder. The ice was cracking!

The surface below me suddenly buckled, shifted, lurched! Water surged up between Metro and me and the men with the empty sleds. The newcomers whirled and whipped their horses back toward the bank.

Metro's horses were alongside the opening crack. He lashed them with his whip, and they cleared the break at once, pulling him and his sled to safety. His horses bolted across the ice and headed for shore.

I stood up and cracked my whip over my terrified team. The bobbing ice floe we were on was starting to sink! "Hey, Tom, hey, Queen!" I shouted, trying to get them to cross to the higher, solid area. Our island of ice was sinking deeper, now maybe ten inches lower than the main surface and separating fast. We were tilting forward. At any moment we could capsize and plunge into the icy water.

The horses went wild. They reared and whinnied. In their terror, they refused to move from the frigid water now bubbling up over their hooves.

Desperately I tried to pull out the connecting pin. Free of our load, the horses—and I—might make it to safety. And then my voice rang out over the ice. "God, help me—please, God, help me!"

There was an incredible lurch. I looked up to see Tom—Tom, the placid horse who minutes before had seemed almost too tired to go anywhere—lunge across that icy gulf and up onto the higher shelf of ice. Never before, never since, have I seen a horse empowered with such super strength. Tom pulled Queen, and me, and the loaded sled with him. And as his hooves hit the other side, our sinking block of ice rose up for a split second, just high enough to let our sled slide across to the firm ice before it smashed back to a level that would have made our crossover impossible.

Tom and Queen took off at a full gallop for the shore while I held tight, praying to God all the while. In front of me were no longer a gray mare and a red gelding, but two whirlwinds fleeing in terror. They hit the bank and clattered over the rocky land, the sled almost breaking up on impact. "Whoa, Tom, whoa, Queen, easy now; we're safe, we're safe." The horses stopped and I tumbled from the sled and threw my arms around their necks. Tom was trembling something awful. I patted him. "Steady, old fella, steady." Whatever, I wondered, had made him do such an incredible thing? And as I asked the question, I knew the answer: I had shouted to God for help and He had heard me. And terrified old Tom had taken us for the leap of his life.

Five days later as Metro and I plodded closer to home, I worried about the reception I'd be receiving. My father had urged me not to go, had cautioned that it might be dangerous. And here I was arriving days later than I'd promised, with animals I had nearly killed and a sled I had battered badly. In addition, it was clear from all the other fishermen at Primrose Lake that there'd be a glut of fish on the market. I wasn't returning home as a triumphant moneymaker—but as a tired, nearly drowned boy with a mess of unwanted fish on his hands.

I felt sheepish and humble as we finally clopped up to the big log farmhouse. Everybody rushed out to greet us. Momma kept shaking her head as she listened to our story, and then she began to cry softly. "Thank God, you're home safely," she said.

My father looked at me thoughtfully. As I stared at him, wondering what kind of a stern reproach he was going to utter, his eyes filled with tears. And then my father reached out and drew me to him. "You're home," he said with a sigh of relief, "home in time for Christmas."

And what a Christmas it was! Mother made delicacies from her native Ukraine. There were special breads, some of them sparkling with sugar—a rare treat for children who usually ate their porridge with salt. There were steaming hot dumplings studded with plump blueberries that had been canned the autumn before; there were buns crisp with poppy seeds. And, of course, a huge, golden turkey.

Relatives and friends arrived in sleighs with bells jingling in the icy air. Inside, everyone gathered around a fragrant tree decked with pine cones and garlands of fleecy wool—from our own sheep—while my father read the story of the nativity from the big family Bible. Then he prayed, thanking God for the gift of His heavenly Son, and asking God's blessing on each of Dad's own children, all fifteen of us. "And especially, God," he said, "thank You for the safe return of Alex."

Several more years were to pass before I surrendered my life completely to Christ and went into full-time Christian service as an evangelist.

But that was the Christmas that I received an abundance of gifts. Those little brown bags were passed out as usual—and how I treasured them. Gold, frankincense, and myrrh could not have been more welcome, for the life that once had seemed so poor now glowed with the richness that had always been there.

Yet the greatest gift of all that Christmas, the one that I've held close all my life, came to me in that moment of desperation on the sinking ice floe—the knowledge that God was not just some strict Being who kept me from having fun on Sundays, but a real God, a God who cared enough to help a struggling boy the day the ice broke.

Comforting Presence

The implications of the name Immanuel are comforting.... Comforting, because He has come to share the danger as well as the drudgery of our everyday lives. He desires to weep with us and to wipe away our tears. And... Jesus Christ, the Son of God, longs to share in and to be the source of the laughter and the joy we all too rarely know.

MICHAEL CARD

Gold, Circumstance, & Mud

BY REX KNOWLES

I t was the week before Christmas.

I was baby-sitting our four older children while my wife took the baby for his check-up. (Baby-sitting to me means reading the paper while the kids mess up the house.)

Only that day I wasn't reading. I was fuming. On every page of the paper, as I flicked angrily through them, gifts glittered and reindeer pranced, and I was told that there were only six more days in which to rush out and buy what I couldn't afford and nobody needed. What, I asked myself indignantly, did the glitter and the rush have to do with the birth of Christ?

There was a knock on the door of the study where I had barricaded myself. Then Nancy's voice: "Daddy, we have a play to put on. Do you want to see it?"

I didn't. But I had fatherly responsibilities so I followed her into the living room. Right away I knew it was a Christmas play, for at the foot of the piano stool was a lighted flashlight wrapped in swaddling clothes lying in a shoe box.

Rex (age six) came in wearing my bathrobe and carrying a mop handle. He sat on the stool, looked at the flashlight. Nancy (ten), a sheet draped over her head, stood behind Rex and began,

"I'm Mary and this boy is Joseph. Usually in this play Joseph stands up and Mary sits down. But Mary sitting down is taller than Joseph standing up so we thought it looked better this way."

Enter Trudy (four) at a full run. She never has learned to walk. There were pillowcases over her arms. She spread them wide and said only, "I'm an angel."

Then came Anne (eight). I knew right away she represented a wise man. In the first place, she moved like she was riding a camel (she had on her mother's high heels). And she was bedecked with all the jewelry available. On a pillow she carried three items, undoubtedly gold, frankincense, and myrrh.

She undulated across the room, bowed to the flashlight, to Mary, to Joseph, to the angel, and to me, and then announced, "I am all three wise men. I bring precious gifts: gold, circumstance, and mud."

That was all. The play was over. I didn't laugh. I prayed. How near the truth Anne was! We come at Christmas burdened down with gold—with the showy gift and the tinselly tree. Under the circumstances we can do no other, circumstances of our time and place and custom. And it seems a bit like mud when we think of it.

But I looked at the shining faces of my children, as their audience of one applauded them, and remembered that a child showed us how these things can be transformed. I remembered that this child came into a material world and, in so doing, eternally blessed the material. He accepted the circumstances, imperfect and frustrating, into which He was born, and thereby infused them with the divine. And as for mud—to you and me it may be something to sweep off the rug, but to all children it is something to build with.

Children see so surely through the tinsel and the habit and the earthly, to the love that, in them all, strains for expression.

Gifts from the Heart

At this special time of year:
Follow the children.
Hear the joy in their laughter.
See the love in their eyes.
Feel the hope in their touch.

Adele

BY NED WALDMAN

Many years ago I published a little book by Tom Hegg called *A Cup of Christmas Tea*. It's a poem about a young man who reluctantly accepts an elderly aunt's holiday invitation. To his surprise, the visit reawakens all the wonderful feelings Christmas had stirred in him as a child—faith, warmth, comfort, the joy of sharing—which he may have lost along the way to adulthood. When Tom first read *A Cup of Christmas Tea* to me, I broke down and wept. I'm Jewish, and sometimes people are surprised that I could be so moved by a Christmas story, or even relate to it at all. "I know all about Christmas," I told Tom. As a little boy, I had celebrated the holiday with someone I loved dearly. She even made special tea on Christmas Eve. Her name was Adele Molitor and, in a way, she was my mom.

You see, my biological mom died in 1933 when I was just six months old. She'd contracted a staph infection. Sadly, penicillin wasn't available in those days. In the depths of despair, my heartbroken father moved to California, leaving my older brother and me behind in Minnesota. My brother went to live with our aunt. I was entrusted to Adele. She'd been our housekeeper and my nanny but now made her living ironing blouses for a local manufacturer. Adele worked hard, but she lavished attention on me. Not a single day went by without her saying, "I love you," in her wonderfully sweet but raspy voice. I remember being very small and looking up into her gentle brown eyes. What did I see? Love, of course. Pure, absolute love.

Adele raised me until I was six, and she respected my Jewish heritage. Still, I enjoyed accompanying her once a week to the Basilica of Saint Mary, a magnificent church that's now a Minneapolis landmark. Its grandeur was a stark contrast to the tiny, one-room apartment we lived in right in the church's shadow, but it never felt intimidating—only comforting. Hundreds of glowing prayer candles tempered the coolness of all that marble and stone. The vaulted ceilings and high dome amplified every whisper. I felt a sacred sense of quietude there.

Nothing brings memories of Adele back to me like Christmastime. Oh, how she loved Christmas, and how she loved for others to share in her joy. Especially me! Since money was so tight, she'd wait till the last possible moment on a Christmas Eve to buy a tree, when the prices had gone down. Invariably, we'd get the skinniest, scraggliest fifty-cent tree you could imagine! But it didn't matter to us if a few branches were missing. We carried it back home through the freezing, snow-covered streets of Minneapolis, dragged it up the stairs, and set it up in the corner so you couldn't see its sparsest side. Adele went over to the old stove and put up a pot of her special Christmas tea, fragrant with cinnamon and cloves and orange peel.

Once the tea was ready, Adele climbed up on a ladder to get the boxes stacked high in the closet and pass them down to me. In them, Adele kept all kinds of Christmas tree ornaments, and all of them were beautiful to me. But my very favorite was a little plush brown bear. "Go on, Ned," she'd say to me, "put Teddy anywhere on the tree, anywhere you like." I felt like the luckiest kid in the whole wide world. We capped off each Christmas Eve listening to the incomparable Kate Smith singing "Silent Night." To this day, it is my favorite song. It's clear to me why those beautiful words, telling the story of a mother and child, so captivated me. I never really knew my mother, but I knew what it was to be loved by a mother—to feel cared for and protected from all the bad things that can happen in this world. In Adele's tender care, all was calm, all was bright.

When I was six, my relatives decided it was time for me to live with my family and learn the traditions of my faith. But even when I grew up and had my own children, I took them to Adele's for Christmas. She never had children of her own and had continued to work very hard and live simply in her small apartment. Since I'd become successful in the book business, I picked out the nicest, fullest tree I could find. No more scraggly fifty-cent trees! She chided me about it. "Ned, you shouldn't spend so much money! We were always happy with those little trees!" She was right. But she'd given me so much. How could I not give back?

When Adele passed away, I felt her loss so deeply. But because of her I published a book that went on to sell millions of copies. Did I know Christmas? Oh yes, I did. And when you know Christmas, you want to pass that gift along to everyone so they will know it too.

Christmas Warmth

The most vivid memories of Christmases past are usually not of gifts given or received, but of the spirit of love, the special warmth of Christmas worship, the cherished little habits of the home, the results of others acting in the spirit of Christ.

LOIS RAND

Stop, Look, & Listen

BY SUE MONK KIDD

It was the day of the Christmas party at the children's home, but my heart wasn't in it. In fact, throughout the holidays I'd found myself going through the motions of Christmas—buying gifts, trimming the tree, even listening to the Christmas story—without much awareness. Once again the holiday had become clouded with shopping, cooking, and a host of wearying details.

"Christmas just isn't what it used to be," I muttered, remembering the wonder-filled Christmases of my childhood.

"Christmas doesn't change," said my husband. "We do."

I shrugged away his comment, thinking of the party. I was to bring a gift for six-year-old Angela, a new child at the home. I'd bought her a nice sensible sweater. Now I wished I'd chosen something else—a doll or a teddy bear. That's when I noticed the little manger made of Popsicle sticks lying in a box of our decorations. On impulse I tucked it in the box with the sweater.

Later that day, Angela shook the gift in eager anticipation. Finally she tore off the wrapping and gazed at the manger.

"It's to remind you that God came to earth as a baby," I explained.

Her eyes widened. She leaped to her feet, paper and ribbon scattering. "God was the baby?"

"Why, yes," I said, realizing this must be the first time she'd heard the Christmas message.

Then Angela did what I suppose all of us should do at such stupendous news. She threw her arms in the air and whirled about, joy dancing all over her. And all of a sudden it was as if I had never heard the story before either.

That year I learned that to make Christmas wonderful we must be full of wonder ourselves. My husband was right. Christmas doesn't change, only people's ability to capture its mystery and marvel. So if you find it difficult to keep the wonder of Christmas kindled amid the fuss and familiarity of the holidays, maybe you'd like to try these helps. They worked for me.

1. Stop, look, and listen. When you discover yourself becoming dulled to the joys of the season, stop. Slow down the pace and grow still, making time to look and listen. Take a winter walk or curl up before the fireplace. Helen Keller once observed, "The seeing see little." So peel familiarity from the glow of a candle and the red of a poinsettia. Listen anew to laughter and bells, and the whisper of love deep in the Bethlehem story.

2. Find ways to anticipate Christ's coming. Our family keeps an Advent calendar during December. Sometimes we hang homemade symbols of Christmas on a tree, counting down the days. One of my favorites is carrying out our "24 ways to

celebrate Advent." Each day we open an envelope on the tree and find a suggestion such as, *Write someone and express your gratitude, forgive an old hurt, tell someone you love him, name your blessings.*

3. Free your childlike spirit. Jesus held up childlikeness as a quality to be cultivated (Mark 10:15). Children dream up simple delights that most of us never experience. There was the year I came upon a little boy singing "Jingle Bells" to a plastic Jesus that was for sale in a department store. And why not? For often Christmas comes in moments such as these, when we enter with spontaneity, with unabashed adoration for the Baby.

4. Be willing to be surprised. Recognize that God comes in the least likely ways. A Holy Child born in a village barn, a strangely lit star, angel song in a night sky. Watch for Him to come in equally surprising ways to you. When we live as if God is going to surprise us any time, any place, any way, He usually does.

5. Share the spirit of Christmas with someone else. Nothing multiplies the sense of wonder in your life like giving it away. The more you share, the brighter Christmas grows. Even if all you have to give is a rickety Popsicle-stick manger.

Not long after that Christmas, Angela left the children's home for a foster family. But hardly a year passes that I don't remember how she awakened me to God's tidings of great joy. And sometimes, too, I smile at the appropriateness of her name.

A Sense of Wonder

It is good to be children sometimes,
and never better than at Christmas,
when its mighty Founder
was a child Himself.

CHARLES DICKENS

A Time for Imagination

BY COMTESSE M. DE LA RIVIERE

In 1944 my mother and I were two of the sixty-four women that the Nazis held prisoner in a small stable in Ludenburg, Germany. The other women were Jews and we were the only Christians; yet, as Christmas approached, Mother and I felt we had to do something to celebrate the holiday.

"We're going to have a Christmas tree," Mother announced to me suddenly on Advent Sunday. Then she outlined her plan, a plan that would have to be carried out in secret.

On Christmas Eve the other women watched with fascination as we produced a strange collection of treasures and began to "make" a Christmas tree. First there was a long pole that I had found in the barn and had kept hidden under my bed. To this we tied the small pine branches snipped from scraggly trees once destined for the wood pile. An empty tin can, laboriously cut apart and shaped, became our "Star of Bethlehem."

For decorations we made bows out of oddments of colored yarn and festoons cut, kindergarten-style, from scraps of paper. Often, after air raids, we had found long silvery threads on the ground. These now served to wrap our tree in gossamer. At last, after each item had been tied on and in place, we felt that there was still something missing.

"Candles," Mother said. "If only we had some candles."

And immediately it came to me where I could find some—the three lanterns in the pig sty. I crept into the Pig's Villa (we called it that because the accommodations were better than ours) and sliced off a good, but not too noticeable, chunk from each candle.

Now our tree came alive. Its light danced in the eyes of all the women who crowded around it as Mother took out her precious New Testament and read aloud the message of good cheer. Then, softly we began to sing the old carols, ending with "Stille Nacht, Heilige Nacht."

Suddenly the door swung open and in strode Max Wagner, a prison officer.

"What is this?" he demanded roughly.

"It is Christmas Eve," said Mother mildly. "We are celebrating the Holy Evening."

"You Jews?" he asked incredulously.

"My daughter and I are Christians."

"You're no different. You have Jewish blood."

"So did the first Christians," Mother replied firmly. "Christianity is a matter of faith, not race."

Furious, Wagner grabbed our tree, tore it apart, and threw the remains in a corner. Then he stomped out, shutting off the lights.

Later, in the darkness, I stretched out my hand to my mother's hand searching from the bunk below. "We had our Christmas," she whispered.

That evening, we knew for a certainty that Christmas, no matter how or with what it is celebrated, is eternal. But that particular Christmas was made unforgettable by a tree created out of our imagination.

Unlimited Celebration

Everywhere, everywhere, Christmas tonight!
Christmas in lands of the fir-tree and pine,
Christmas in lands of the palm-tree and vine...
Christmas where peace, like a dove in his flight,
Broods o'er brave men in the thick of the fight;
Everywhere, everywhere, Christmas tonight!

PHILLIPS BROOKS

A Very English Christmas

BY BARBARA HAMPTON

It was to be different, that Christmas of 1984. For our family of five, on sabbatical from the College of Wooster in Ohio, the season held promise of a traditional British Christmas with Yule logs, plum puddings, and carols sung in stately chapels. It would be a season when I'd abandon my fear of pastry and bake those tangy mince pies that all of England eats on Christmas Day. It would be a classic, "proper" holiday.

We were spending the year in Cambridge, that glorious English town whose history reaches back to prehistoric times and whose university had its beginnings in the thirteenth century on the banks of the River Cam northeast of London. The mathematician and philosopher Sir Isaac Newton, and the poets Milton, Coleridge, Tennyson, Byron, and Wordsworth were scholars at the colleges, whose ornate gates bear the insignia of royal benefactors.

The very unroyal Oliver Cromwell, who overthrew the monarchy for a five-year term, studied here in 1616 at Sidney Sussex College; and the very royal and current Prince Charles read history at Trinity College, chartered in 1546 by King Henry VIII. Here too my husband, Chuck, was studying (the philosophy of mathematics) and climbing creaking staircases and searching library shelves for works of some of the same men who, years before, had come here to learn.

As Christmas approached, damp cold and fog rolled in from the Fens, the flat, low-lying farm country to the north. Buttoned up against the chill, Chuck and I and our daughters, Jenny, twelve, Ellen, nine, and Karen, seven, browsed in the open-air market in search of Yuletide remembrances.

We trudged along Market Street, then down Peas Hill, where soon the girls would be attending "Jack and the Beanstalk" at the Arts Theatre. Fairy tales pantomimed onstage at Christmastime usher in the season for British children, and our three eagerly awaited the comical songs and audience participation that their schoolmates were treated to each December.

Glancing across King's Parade to the great spires of Wing's College, I mused on the festival of song for which choirboys were at that moment practicing—their voices lifting up and up to the awe-inspiring eighty-foot, fan-vaulted chapel ceiling dating back to 1515. The festival of nine lessons and carols has been held annually since 1918 and is broadcast around the world by BBC. With its opening solo, "Once in Royal David's City," all of Britain commences to trim its trees. The service, after all, is central to the meaning of the season.

Our family would be listening to the live radio broadcast at 3:00 p.m. on Christmas Eve in our tiny rowhouse on Mulberry Close. Or so I thought.

All too quickly our dreams of a quaint, heartwarming Victorian Christmas, the kind that Dickens would approve, were shattered. Two weeks before Christmas, Karen, our youngest and most vulnerable (the "Tiny Tim" of our family), had to be hospitalized because of a mysterious lung infection that became worse with each day. She lay unresponsive, close to death.

Throughout the town, holly boughs and ivy garlands wound around mahogany balustrades and down ancient banisters to proclaim that Christmas had come. Silver stars and tinsel streamers joined hanging red balls in shop windows to echo the message. Here and there, Norwegian spruces, clamped in stands, announced it in homes. Schoolchildren worked furiously on varicolored paper chains that fathers and uncles would be draping across ceilings as the Birthday drew near. And the ubiquitous red postal trucks braved traffic jams to bring the news by mail—to be enjoyed during Britain's favorite afternoon break over hot tea and scones.

None of this was ours as we waited anxiously by Karen's bedside, playing her favorite tapes, reading her stories, hoping to pull her back from unconsciousness, back to life. Chuck skipped classes, and Jenny and Ellen skipped Christmasing to run errands and do laundry between their lessons. Christmas remained a stranger.

As we watched over Karen in the children's ward of Addenbrooke's modern research hospital, named for a Cambridge graduate, Chuck reminded me, "This is one of the best hospitals in the country. She's in good care."

But that was not comfort enough. I needed more—I needed to know that God was not abandoning us this year, that He would not be taking away my baby of the soft brown curls and small, painfully pale frame. And in between the repetition of ditties and rhymes, I worried alongside other parents hovering over sick children in the ward. To be so far from home, so far from family....

But then, God's assurance did begin flowing onto that hospital ward. It came in a flood of cards and mince pies and casserole suppers and a Christmas cactus. It was brought in the hands of our neighbors on the Close, by fellow students at Wolfson College, by communicants from our church away from home, The Round Church, a Norman building of rounded arches and zigzag moldings constructed by the Knights Templar about 1130. It arrived with the providential presence of the only doctor we knew, a member of our Bible study group, as Karen was being wheeled into emergency surgery.

It came with the prayers of the Free Church chaplain, who stood by Karen's bed the next day. She responded by opening her eyes for the first time and telling us weakly, "When I grow up, I want to be a nurse."

That moment was my Christmas gift from God. He had given back my child, and from that day Karen began improving. And in God's sometimes humorous way, He gave Karen a gift as well, a doll from Father Christmas, who visited the ward on Christmas morning.

"Baby Skates!" whispered Karen as she took the doll from the red-robed, red-hooded man of gift-giving fame. "Look, Mama—Baby Skates!"

I could only sigh and smile in resignation. Chuck and I had resisted yet longed for this particular doll. "Karen, Jesus must have told Father Christmas that you wanted Baby Skates," was all I could reply. And now here we were, stuck with a Baby Skates!

But then, we had been looking at life through adult eyes—sophisticated, in search of knowledge, desirous of an excellent education for our children and aware of images and traditions. Perhaps God wanted us to see and celebrate His birth as children, to adore Him as children. Perhaps He wanted to break through the images with the reality of His gift to us. Perhaps that is why He sent us that year to the children's ward of Addenbrooke's Hospital, where we gathered with other families around a Christmas table laden with stuffed turkey, potatoes and Brussels sprouts, *chipolatas* (small sausages), tangerines, and, yes, Mrs. Cratchit's pride: a plum pudding graced by a twig of holly.

And it was in the spirit of childhood that we pulled our "crackers," bright paper favors that go *bang* when opened, donned our silly holiday hats, and listened to the Queen's annual Christmas Day message.

The Queen's words of hope and peace carried a reminder at the end, which she quoted from the Bible: "Except ye...become as little children, ye shall not enter into the kingdom of heaven" (Matthew 18:3).

In all of the pomp and ceremony of life at Cambridge, in its magnificent structures by Christopher Wren and William Morris and noted craftsmen from around the world, Jesus had brought us once again to the lowly manger and the Christ child, who reigns over all.

The Majesty of Christmas

Come now with joy to worship and adore Him;
hushed in the stillness, wonder and behold
Christ in the stable where His mother bore him,
Christ whom the prophets faithfully foretold:
High King of ages, low we kneel before Him,
starlight for silver, and lantern-light for gold.

TIMOTHY DUDLEY-SMITH

Our Light in the Night

BY MARGARET PEGRAM MORRISON

When I was a child there was always an evening in late November when Daddy would say to Momma, "What do you think? Sunday after this one coming up is the first Sunday of Advent. Isn't it time to start our star?" Without waiting for an answer, all three of us children would jump up to clear the dishes. Daddy would put the extra leaf in the table, and Momma would get out white paper, cardboard patterns, and the blunt-end scissors. It was time to make our Moravian star.

We lived in Winston-Salem, North Carolina, and because the town of Salem was first settled by members of the Moravian church, we celebrated many of their customs. In their churches the Moravian stars were hung, but we made one for our own front porch.

Every night for a week the scene after supper was the same. We traced the patterns, cut and folded and glued until we had finished all of the star's twenty-six fragile points. Sometimes Daddy read the Christmas story as we worked. Sometimes he talked about how the wise men of today still need a light to guide them. Momma helped when a fold went crooked and wiped up sticky smudges where small hands put more paste on the table than on the paper.

Making each point was tedious work. The seams were so small it was hard for us to get them folded straight. When one of the points was misshapen, Momma or Daddy asked, "Would you feel better if you did it over?" We children would decide whether the point was worthy of going onto the star. And each night the row of points placed on the sideboard to dry grew longer.

One evening when we were nearing the end, my little sister called, "Finished! Finished!" But then she bumped the table with the very last point and crushed it as she was taking it over to dry. She began to cry, but Momma took over, bending the point until it began to straighten. Then my brother exclaimed, "We have to cut one anyway to put in the light. That point can be the one that lights the star!"

The smile that Momma and Daddy exchanged lit the room. Daddy had rigged a socket on a short electrical cord. The broken end of the point was cut off and the cord threaded through. Then we all went out to the front porch and watched proudly as Daddy hung the star and turned on the light.

What a glorious light it was. As a matter of fact, when placed inside the Christmas star, the same bulb that the rest of the year was just bright enough to light our way up the porch steps was so brilliant it was visible more than a block away. It hardly seemed possible, but our homemade star lit up the neighborhood.

Perhaps grown-up hands patched up our work after we had gone to bed. Perhaps those same hands repaired the joints in the star when they came loose. All I know is that year after year, whether there was snow or sleet, that fragile creation made of white paper and flour-and-water paste lasted from the first Sunday of Advent to Epiphany.

No matter how wide it swung in the night wind, it was whole and still shining the next morning. Nowadays the stars are made of durable plastic and are available in kits. Each year when I hang my sturdy holiday star, I close my eyes and see the stars of my childhood. I picture us gathered around them to declare this year's creation the best one ever!

And I still hear Momma and Daddy as they prayed that each of us might strive to be worthy so that the light of the star could say, "You will find God present here."

Seeking the Light

*Lord Jesus, Master of both the Light
and the darkness, send Your Holy Spirit
upon our preparations for Christmas.
We who have so much to do seek quiet spaces
to hear Your voice each day.
We who are anxious about many things look
forward to Your coming among us....
We are Your people, walking in darkness,
yet seeking the light.
To You we say, "Come, Lord Jesus!"*

HENRI J. M. NOUWEN

Shining Through

I n our nightly dinner table reading of the Advent calendar, the wise men were almost to Bethlehem. It was fifteen-year-old Sanna's turn to read aloud, and she was flying through it as if she couldn't get them to the manger fast enough. I gritted my teeth as her younger brother, Jonathan, stared at her comically, his victory complete when Sanna lost her concentration and dissolved into giggles. Laura, our seventeen-year-old, seemed to be above it all, chewing quietly.

It's not the same anymore, I brooded, trying to cap my disappointment. Our house used to be full of Christmas spirit. But the kids weren't as wrapped up anymore in the old traditions they once cherished, like reading the Advent calendar every night.

After dinner I returned the calendar to the refrigerator door and loaded the dishwasher, daydreaming about the annual Christmas pageant the kids used to put on for Whitney and me. I'd let them raid the linen closet for costumes. One year our scruffy black dog was the third wise man. Her tail drooped in embarrassment through her bed-sheet getup. Now I glanced at her as she waddled, old and stiff, across the kitchen to her bowl, and I wondered if she remembered too.

Things picked up a little the next day when our oldest, Wendy, returned from college. "It's me!" her voice erupted as she banged through the kitchen door, gorged luggage skidding across the linoleum. I call Wendy my whirlwind child. I was forever telling her to slow down and think—generally to no avail. But Whitney and I were grateful for her impulsive generosity when she treated her brother and sisters to dinner out that night. It gave us time to apply the final holiday touches at home. The house was spotless and smelled of lemon and pine and fresh-baked pies. I wanted to give my best for the coming of the Christ child.

When Whitney finally flicked on the tree lights, I felt the stirrings of the old Christmas spirit. "There," I sighed, leaning against him, "perfect."

The next night was Christmas Eve. The house buzzed with all of us getting dressed for church. Whitney, Jonathan, and I were going to the five o'clock service. My daughters preferred the later one. Between, we'd meet at a restaurant for dinner. "See you at seven, girls," Whitney called as we left. Just before I tugged the front door shut I turned for a last look at our handiwork. *Yes, it really is beginning to feel like Christmas.*

The five o'clock service was boisterous. Nervous mothers helped small children into costumes. I felt a stab of envy, remembering when I helped ready my little ones for the pageant. I felt tired from all the hard work the holidays demand. The lights dimmed and the little stage became a stable. The simplicity of it reminded me of how stark that first Christmas had actually been, how transient. The scene closed with an enormous glitter-covered star leading the wise men to the manger, where they knelt with their gifts. We all sang "We Three Kings of Orient Are" and it was over.

Whitney pulled into the restaurant parking lot, and my eyes quickly scanned the cars for Wendy's beat-up old Dodge. We went inside. Rotund candles burned in pine wreaths on the tables. Christmas music spilled from concealed speakers. Where were my girls?

The waiter seated us at a window table. I was grateful to have a view of the lot so that I could stop worrying the minute the old Dodge made an appearance. When it finally did, irritation and relief battled for control of my feelings. Then I saw the girls' glum faces as they filed by the window and came inside.

They took their seats silently. I wasn't sure I wanted to hear the explanation I knew was coming. "Mom," Wendy began, knotting a green napkin that proclaimed MERRY CHRISTMAS, "there's been a fire, just a tiny fire in the kitchen, but it made a lot of soot."

The menu fell out of my hands. "How much soot?"

Then Wendy was crying, huge rolling tears I hadn't seen her shed in years. She'd been melting some wax to do her legs and in her typical haste she thought she'd turned off the burner but in fact hadn't. That's how the pan caught fire. "At least the house didn't burn up," Laura offered, looking for that silver lining in a very dark cloud.

"Thank God you guys are all safe," said Whitney.

"I'm really sorry, Mom," Wendy gulped.

The minute we walked in the house the choking stench of soot hit me. The downstairs was a disaster—ceilings, walls, furniture, Christmas decorations, the nativity set—all overlaid with a grimy black film. I swung open the cupboards and slammed them shut. The soot had gotten in there too, on our dishes and silverware, our spice tins and canned goods. My pies were ruined. The soles of our shoes turned black from the floor. My hands were black.

On the refrigerator the Advent calendar with the picture of the wise men was black...the star too, as if it had burned out. And for me it had. We retreated upstairs and spent the night in the house. But the smell of smoke was so bad, and the kitchen virtually unusable, that the next morning we had to abandon our home. Christmas morning.

The only place we could find to have dinner was a hotel coffee shop. We just didn't feel up to horning in on friends. "This is kind of like no room at the inn," Whitney commented as we ate hamburgers.

"Yeah," Laura agreed eagerly, "I guess things fell apart in Bethlehem too." My husband grinned and my children laughed—and I tried, I really tried, to join in. But the anger wouldn't leave me. Wendy had apologized. She felt terrible and had learned a lesson, she informed me. I'd said I forgave her. The insurance company would pay for everything, even our hotel bill, until the downstairs could be cleaned and painted. Yet in my heart I struggled with resentment that seemed to grow larger every time I thought about our ruined Christmas. Ruined.

The next day we were all going to go bowling together. I just couldn't. "You go," I told Whitney. "I need some time." Wendy gave me a squeeze as they filed out the door.

After they'd gone I threw on a coat and headed for the house, thinking that I'd take down some of the decorations and clean them off as best I could. I needed to do something.

Fog and drizzle hid the house till I was in the drive. Inside, the air still reeked of smoke. If anything, even more of the wretched soot had settled. The place was stale and depressing. I'd made a mistake in coming.

I began taking the decorations off the tree, wiping them delicately with a rag. Soon my hands were pitch black, my nose was clogged. Was this really the same perfect room where I'd stood with Whitney and felt the coming of Christmas?

The ornament slid from my fingertips as tears filled my eyes and carved rivulets down my sooty cheeks. I'd had a feeling about this Christmas. Even before the fire. The kids seemed different—older, jaded. No one cared much about all the lovely holiday trappings I held so dear. I pulled myself to a chair and collapsed.

Then my eyes landed on the crèche. Instinctively I reached out with one hand while trying to smear away my messy tears with the other. I plucked the baby Jesus from His crib. He lay in the palm of my hand, gray with soot, ruined, just like everything else in the room, like everything else this Christmas. I wiped the figurine on my old denim shirtsleeve. My teardrops helped clear away some of the dirt. I wiped a little more. And more. I wanted at least this one thing to be clean, to be perfect. Soon the Christ child shone.

And then I began to feel it, finally, for the first time that year, the spirit of Christmas. Amazing, I thought, how this little figure, wiped clean, shines through it all.

There were no decorations when He came down from heaven that first Christmas. The world was a mess, wildly imperfect, just as it is today. But that didn't prevent God's love for us from bursting through in Bethlehem.

Christmases are never the same. They change from year to year, and they are never really perfect, no matter how hard we try to force them to be so. What is perfect is the miracle in Bethlehem two thousand years ago and the love of God that continues to burst through the chaos of human imperfection. Christmas is finding the Christ child radiant beneath the daily grime of life.

With a prayer of thanks I carefully replaced the Infant in the manger. The rest of the cleanup could wait. I had to find Whitney and the kids. I knew they'd probably be eating hamburgers at the hotel coffee shop. I couldn't wait to join them.

Worth Having

The magical dust of Christmas glittered on the cheeks of humanity ever so briefly, reminding us of what is worth having and what we were intended to be.

MAX LUCADO

Empty Manger

BY MARY ANN O'ROARK

W*here is he?* I rummaged through the box. The Christ child was missing—just when I'd decided that putting up the nativity scene my parents brought me from the Holy Land would finally get me into the Christmas mood.

As soon as I had gotten home from the office I had pulled out the box from the back of my closet and had dug into the bundles of tissue paper. Two sheep of gold-brown wood, three stately wise men and a leggy camel, an ox and donkey and a stable with a star. Then came Joseph and Mary. But the baby Jesus was missing. Forget setting up the crèche. I'd sit Christmas out this year.

The next morning I headed to work, my head down and hands thrust into my coat pockets, as if steeling myself for the onslaught of decorated store windows and tourists loaded down with red and green shopping bags. Somehow this year I was feeling not only melancholy but overwhelmed and cynical. Had I simply grown immune to the annual epidemic of Christmas spirit?

That's when I saw her—the woman with the grimy green hat. She'd become a regular on my block, slouched and smoking in a doorway, or digging through a trash can. I guessed she slept at a homeless shelter, though occasionally I saw her sprawled on the steps of a nearby stone church. I'd volunteered in a soup kitchen for years and usually wasn't put off by street people. But this woman was hard to take, cursing passersby and shouting at cars. That day she lurched in front of me, thrusting out a swollen hand. "Got any money?" she rasped.

"No," I snapped. She took a step closer and I quickly crossed the street to get away from her. I found myself directly in front of the church. In a small concrete courtyard set off by a wrought-iron railing was the beautiful manger scene they put up every year. Wise men, shepherds, a man in a robe, and a woman in blue all gazed down at a wooden manger filled with straw. And centered in the hay, plump arms open, lay a plaster baby Jesus. A halo curved around his head in a golden crescent, swaddling clothes covered his infant midriff. Here was baby Jesus, in the midst of corner delis and shoe stores, the hustle and bustle of city life flowing around him like a river.

I stopped and took it all in. For a fleeting instant I almost felt the old spark of Christmas. Then I heard her, the bag lady, yelling and cursing. Well, at least two of us in this city didn't have the spirit of the season in our hearts.

Yet over the following days I found myself passing by the church's crèche again, drawn perhaps to the simple, ancient scene to help make up for the incomplete one I refused to put up in my apartment.

I'd once written an article about Saint Francis of Assisi, the gentle and visionary monk who had created the first nativity scene in 1223, in a cave on a mountainside in central Italy. At a time when only the wealthy were allowed into the church's inner sanctum, Francis was determined to emphasize the Christ child's peasant birth and pay tribute to the humble animals Francis called "sister and brother." With his friend Giovanni di Velita, the lord of Greccio, Francis set up a simple hay-filled manger in a rocky crevice. Monks tethered an ox and donkey next to the empty crib.

On Christmas Eve worshipers came from miles around and proceeded up the mountain, carrying candles and torches that lit the velvety blackness like a galaxy of stars. The crowds gathered in hushed awe around the scene. Some onlookers reported they actually saw the form of baby Jesus appear on the hay; one observer was sure that the glowing infant opened his eyes and smiled lovingly at Saint Francis.

How real the Christ child was to those people, I thought the next time I passed my neighborhood nativity scene. Here, centuries later, as the winter winds whistled, the absurd thought crossed my mind that the infant, covered only by a painted strip of swaddling clothes, might be cold. *What a crazy idea*, I thought, pulling my coat tighter around me, continuing down the block.

Christmas was only a few days away when I came hurrying up the street one sleety morning. From under my umbrella I glanced at the nativity, then stopped. Mary and Joseph stood vigil, faithful as always—but over an empty manger. There was an indentation in the straw, but no baby.

I didn't know whether I wanted to cry or shout and scream like the bag lady in the green hat. I couldn't believe someone would steal the Christ child! Just like in my crèche at home, this baby was gone too.

The sleet spattered on my umbrella, and I headed down the street feeling completely dejected. Who would do such a dreadful thing? I was almost to the subway when out of the corner of my eye I saw a huddled form in an alley by a parking garage.

Hunched against the wall was the woman in the green hat. But she wasn't cursing or panhandling. She was bent protectively over a bundle in her arms wrapped in a blanket. As she rocked it back and forth, a corner of the blanket fell away and I saw a plump plaster arm, then the curve of a golden halo. Cuddling the infant even closer to her chest, she kissed its painted brow.

I stood watching, and for a split second I had the incredible notion that the baby opened its eyes and smiled up at the hovering woman. Then there was a gust of wind and the woman pulled up the blanket to shelter the baby. I could see her lips moving, and I heard a wisp of drifting melody, raspy but sweet on the frosty air. "Silent night, holy night..."

She never looked up; I never approached her. But I knew without a doubt that the spirit of the Christ child had never been missing. It might be where I least expected it, but it was never far away. That weary woman and those rushing crowds were as much a part of the manger scene as the ungodly chaos and ineffable holiness in the little town of Bethlehem so many centuries ago.

I quickened my pace, then turned one more time before going into the subway station. The woman emerged from the alley and headed back toward the church, the infant figure still held lovingly in her arms and her green hat suddenly vivid against the gray cityscape.

That night the December sky gave way to an enormous white moon. I unwrapped my parents' Holy Land figures and arranged them on my mantel. The missing baby didn't bother me. Like the worshipers in the Middle Ages to whom baby Jesus was so real that they saw him in an empty manger, I too knew His Spirit was present—at the center of not just a single holiday season but of my life.

Love Came Down

God must have said, "I know what I'll do,
I'll send my LOVE right down there where they are.
And I'll send it as a tiny baby, so they'll have
to touch it, and they'll have to hold it close."

GLORIA GAITHER

A Note from the Editors

Guideposts, a nonprofit organization, touches millions of lives every day through products and services that inspire, encourage, and uplift. Our magazines, books, prayer network, and outreach programs help people connect their faith-filled values to their daily lives. To learn more, visit Guideposts.org or GuidepostsFoundation.org.